The History and Natural History of Lugg Meadow

The History and Natural History of Lugg Meadow

by
Anthea Brian & Peter Thomson

with drawings *by* Pat Barbrook
and a section on hay making written
& illustrated *by* Geoff Wilkinson

Anthea Brian
in association with
LOGASTON PRESS

LOGASTON PRESS
Little Logaston, Logaston,
Woonton, Almeley, Herefordshire HR3 6QH

First published by Anthea Brian and Logaston Press 2002

ISBN 1 873827 38 5

Set in Times by Logaston Press
and printed in Great Britain by
Bell & Bain Ltd., Glasgow

Cover illustrations:
Front: Snake's Head Fritillary
Back: (anti-clockwise from top right): A dole stone set up in 1833; Autumn—commoners' sheep on the meadow and the floods begin; Reserve wardens 'set out' the meadow for hay-cutting; Hay-making in progress

Contents

All profits from the sale of this booklet will go to the Herefordshire Conservation Development Trust which helps to fund the purchase of nature reserves in the county by the Herefordshire Nature Trust

Introduction

The casual reader browsing in a bookshop and coming on this booklet may well ask what is so special about this particular meadow that it merits a publication all to itself?

There are many answers to this question. Perhaps that here in spring you can see the rare Fritillary in flower or hear the Curlew call. Perhaps that in summer you can come on real, old-fashioned hay-making in progress and smell the wonderful scent of new-mown hay or perhaps that in a cold winter you can skate or slide on acres and acres of frozen flood water.

But there are three even more important reasons why Lugg Meadow merits a publication to itself.

The first is that it makes up a large part of the very small area of flowery hay meadow that has survived in England as a whole. Only about 5% remains from the intensification of agriculture that we have seen in recent years and Lugg Meadow is a large part of that.

A second reason is that its method of management, which is that of a Lammas meadow, has remained unchanged in essentials from medieval times and probably from long before that. It is in fact the largest surviving Lammas meadow in the whole country and a true example of living history.

The third reason concerns the documentary records of the Meadow. A great many of these have survived in the Cathedral's record office housed in the Mappa Mundi building and these show that the ownership of the Meadow was linked to the Hereford Bishopric and the Cathedral Dignitaries from very early times right up to the last century and that large parts of the Meadow fairly certainly formed a part of the Cathedral's original, pre-conquest endowment of lands.

Lugg Meadow, close to Hereford city, lies beside and has been shaped by the River Lugg whose ancient Celtic name means '*bright stream*'. Over the years the farm animals, the implements and the farmers themselves have changed and modernised but the ancient methods of management have remained the same. As a result Lugg Meadow is today over three hundred acres of ancient hay meadow with the wild flowers, the insects, the birds and other wildlife typical of that habitat still present in a county and in a country where such meadowland has today almost disappeared.

As a nation we carefully cherish our ancient buildings and spend large sums annually on their upkeep. In contrast Lugg Meadow, which is older still, maintains itself at no cost to us and continues to produce an annual crop of valuable hay. In the past this hay was a source of great wealth to those who built and maintained Hereford Cathedral and a landscape historian, writing to emphasise the importance of the Meadow has said:

> Here at Hereford we are not just looking at a pleasant view, or an interesting arrangement of plants. We are looking at an increasingly rare example of an area of land whose management helped to hold together the very fabric of a past society. Without the Lugg Meadows of this world there would have been no Hereford Cathedral, no Mappa Mundi - perhaps not even a Hereford itself.

In this booklet an attempt has been made for the first time to draw together all aspects of Lugg Meadow, its origins, its history and its wildlife, and it is hoped that greater knowledge will lead to a greater interest in the preservation of the Meadow so that future generations may still enjoy what we have today.

1
The Origins of Meadows in the Lower Lugg Valley

When man settled in the Lugg valley he began to clear the trees from the lower, flatter parts near the river but left woodland on the steeper, less accessible slopes. As agriculture developed the grazing flocks would have been herded on the fertile flood-plain land beside the river and in the early days it is thought that these flocks and herds would have come from many settlements. Some of these would have been situated quite far from the river but all grazed their animals together on the riverside pastures. This practice is known as intercommoning and there is evidence that its origins date back to the Bronze Age (*c*.650 BC). Intercommoning continued on meadows in Marden and Sutton up to the 19th century where in addition to local people farmers from parishes such as Preston Wynne, Felton and Little Cowarne had grazing rights as well. To this very day certain farms in Lugwardine, Holmer, Tupsley and Hampton Bishop retain their ancient rights to graze their animals in common on Lugg Meadow.

In the early days the flood-plain grasslands were managed as pasture rather than meadow. A *pasture* is permanent grassland that is managed by regular grazing throughout the growing season. In contrast a *meadow* is permanent grassland that is left ungrazed throughout the growing season so that a crop of hay can be taken. After the hay has been carried a meadow may be grazed until winter comes. In the past any one field was always either a pasture or a meadow and developed a distinctive flora as a result. Modern agricultural practices such as ley-farming and silage cutting have blurred the distinction between meadow and pasture and so has the modern tendency to call any attractive bit of grassland a 'meadow', regardless of its true status. Advertisers of dairy products also use the word freely and have added to the confusion.

To make proper hay some grass-cutting instrument is required and the Romans (*c*.50-400 AD) are the first people known to have had scythes so it seems probable that hay-making began with them. It was certainly well established in the Saxon period (*c*.400-1070 AD) for, by the time the Normans arrived in England, nearly all settlements had their own hay meadows. These were recorded carefully in Domesday Book in 1086 and the meadows of the Lower Lugg valley were then much the largest in the county.

The large size of these meadows resulted from the very wide expanse of flood-plain that existed in this area then and still does today. This in its turn results from a period before the ice ages when a very much larger river flowed in this part of the Lugg valley, a river of which the Wye was at that time a tributary. (The evidence for this is explained in section 6 on the Origins of the Lugg valley landscape).

Meadow land was always valued at a much higher rate than arable land and flood-plain meadows were especially valuable because the annual winter flooding spread natural fertilisers over the grass thus replacing the nutrients removed each year in the hay crop. (All school children used to be taught about the importance of the annual floods of the River Nile to the economy of ancient Egypt but somehow the same phenomenon, taking place each year in this country, completely escaped notice!) The natural advantages conferred by flooding came to a sudden end when artificial fertilisers were introduced and 'bag fertilisers' could be added easily to both arable and pasture land.

By early medieval times (*c*.1070-1350) the open field system of agriculture was widespread over the country. This system was especially associated with the Midlands but existed over most of Herefordshire in some form and was well established in the Lugg valley. Under this system each settlement, consisting of houses with enclosed paddocks around them, was surrounded by land farmed in common by the inhabitants. This land was typically made up of four elements:

1) *Open arable fields*, where corn and other crops were grown, situated near to the settlement.
2) *Woodland*, which provided building timber and firewood, situated on poor ground and steep slopes.
3) *Rough grazing* used all the year round, situated on the poorest ground, known as the 'manorial waste'.
4) A *Meadow*, called the Common or Lammas Meadow, where the hay needed to feed the plough oxen and other stock through the winter was grown. This meadow was situated on the most fertile ground in the parish, normally beside a stream or river. When land was being valued in inventories and other documents meadowland was always given the highest value of all. (The position of these meadows in the settlements of the Lower Lugg valley is shown in Fig.1)

The management of these four different areas was controlled by the manorial court in such a way that the settlement was virtually self-sufficient. The

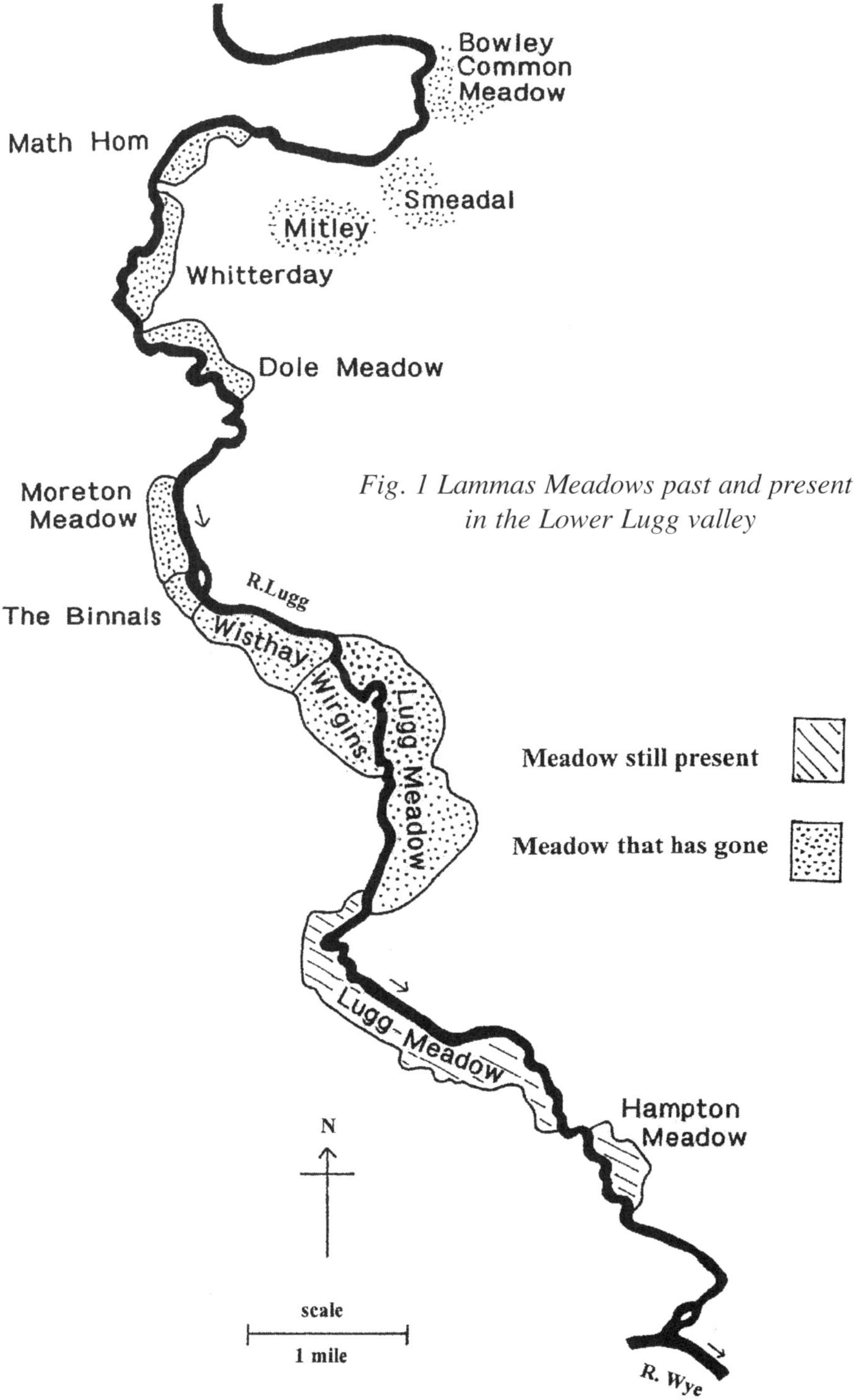

Fig. 1 Lammas Meadows past and present in the Lower Lugg valley

system broke down gradually over the course of time as manorial courts lost their power and in many places the change from communal to private ownership of land was completed by an Enclosure Act in the 17th-19th centuries. The passing of such an Act resulted in land that had previously been held in common being parcelled out into new units in individual ownership. As a result hedges were planted around the newly enclosed fields on former Lammas Meadows and the management of the land often changed from hay meadow to permanent pasture. Some parts of former meadows were drained and ploughed up to grow arable crops. Many of the plants, like the Snake's Head Fritillary that had thrived in the hay meadow, could not survive these changes in management and disappeared completely.

However, in the Lugg Meadow parishes of Lugwardine, Holmer and Tupsley elements of the medieval open field system persisted into the 19th century and Lugwardine and Tupsley never had Enclosure Acts. Instead the arable land was enclosed piecemeal over a long period of time while Lugg Meadow itself was never enclosed and as a result has remained an ancient Common or Lammas meadow with its origins back in Saxon or Dark Age times.

2
The Management of Lugg Meadow

(a) Round the year on Lugg Meadow

Most agricultural fields today change their crops from year to year, from grass to wheat to potatoes and so on so that their aspect is never the same. Lugg Meadow in contrast has a regular unchanging annual cycle based on two dates in the calendar: Candlemas (2 February) and Lammas (1 August). Both of these days are ancient church festivals and their use to control farming activities on Lugg Meadow serves to highlight the ancient origins of the meadow dating back as it does to a period when all aspects of daily life were dated by the church calendar.

Today at any time from Lammas day onward cattle and sheep may be seen grazing on the Meadow until the floods force them to be taken off. These animals belong to farms that have commoner's rights on the Meadow which, as described in section 1, lie mostly in the parishes of Holmer, Lugwardine and Tupsley. The rights are ancient and go with the farm rather than the owner but all had to be registered for the first time in 1965 under the Commons Act.

On the Meadow all aspects of the grazing are controlled by the Commoners Association and the 'Hayward' looks after the welfare of the animals while they are on the meadow. 'Hayward' was the ancient title for the job of the man concerned with the grazing animals and not, as the name suggests, with the hay crop; this was in the hands of the 'Meadsman'. The grazing of the Meadow was controlled by the manorial court which prevented any illegal activities that 'oppressed the commons' and fined wrong-doers. In the absence of a manorial court today a strong commoner's association is vital for the continuance of traditional management of the Meadow.

By 2 February, Candlemas, any remaining animals must be removed from the Meadow and it comes into the hands of the owners.

As regards ownership, the Meadow is divided up by invisible lines into areas of different sizes, some are long, narrow 'strips' and some are irregularly shaped 'parcels'. In the 1840s when these areas were all mapped for the first time there were over 150 of them. Today the strips and parcels are bought and sold like any other land but are always sold subject to the commoner's rights to graze for half the year. Several of the commoners are owners of strips or parcels but there are also owners who are not commoners and *vice versa*.

From Candlemas onwards the Meadow is shut up to grow a crop of hay. While the grass is growing the divisions between strips and parcels cannot be identified except by subtle differences in the grass and the flowers that grow among it. These differences have arisen because parts under different ownership may have been treated differently. Some may have had a dressing of farmyard manure, some, alas, were sprayed with herbicide in the past after which the flowers take some years to recover, some are cut early and some are cut late or, in some years, not cut at all. All this variety of treatment in one meadow makes for a diverse and patchy flora.

The scene changes in late June or early July when hay cutting starts and suddenly the pattern of ownership, visible only on the map till then, becomes visible in the meadow itself. How the owners know just where to cut in the huge area of waving grass was worked out long ago and is a fascinating story

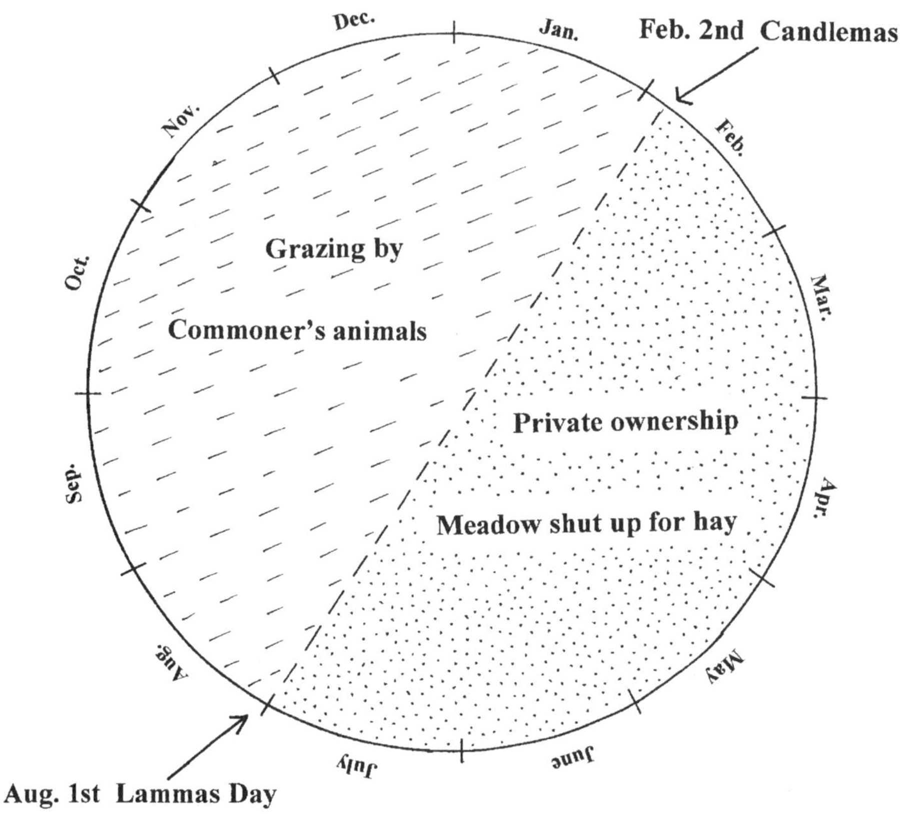

Fig. 2 The yearly cycle on a Lammas Meadow

Two women raking the hay on Lugg Meadow into windrows with the waggon, onto which the hay is being loaded, following on behind. Photo taken by Alfred Watkins, probably around 1900. (Reproduced by courtesy of Hereford Library)

Scything and sharpening a scythe

in its own right which is described in the next section. Once cut the hay makes quickly on the open, breezy Meadow if the weather is good and this is a great benefit, especially to the many owners who come from a distance to make their hay crop.

By Lammas Day all the hay has been carted and the grass has started to grow again forming the 'aftermath'. The Commoners then hold a meeting to decide on what date the animals should be allowed back onto the meadow and the annual cycle begins again. The name 'Lammas Meadow' was given to all such meadows held in common for part of the year because Lammas Day was such a significant date in the annual cycle. These meadows were also sometimes called 'Common Meadow' because of the communal grazing. The two terms are synonymous but Lammas Meadow is the most distinctive and is used in this booklet.

Today we do not celebrate Lammas Day but in medieval times it must have been a time of rejoicing. Before that date, with crops growing on all the arable fields, there were few places where the flocks and herds could be grazed so that the herdsman must have found the animals hard to contain and food was getting in short supply for animals and people alike. Then on Lammas Day the animals could be set free to graze in the Meadow and the people could turn their attention to the all important corn harvest. As a result they celebrated the start of the harvest and they brought the first loaf, made from the newly cut corn, to church to be blessed at the 'Loaf Mass'. As food has become more plentiful the celebration of harvest has shifted to the end of harvest time and the autumn Harvest Festival has come to replace the August Loaf Mass.

(b) Marking the boundaries—dole stones and mere stones

Standing in Lugg Meadow in the long grass just before the hay is cut it appears incredible that anyone can know just where the ownership boundaries that divide the meadow lie. But this is an ancient problem that was solved long ago. Basically two methods are used in conjunction; the approximate position of the corner of a strip is found by lining up two landmarks such as two trees, one on the edge of the meadow and the other on the horizon. When the approximate position has been found a search is made for some marker in the ground. This is usually an upright stone variously called a 'mere' stone ('mere' meaning a boundary), or 'dole' stone (because the strips were sometimes doled out). There are over a hundred such stones on Lugg Meadow today and it is known that not so long ago there were very many more. Some of these are broken or heaped up into piles and some only project a few inches out of the ground but the majority are upstanding and are made of local sandstone. Some may have initials and a date carved on them and most of these appear to date from the 19th century. There is a very good set of stones all marked 'CB 1833' which were put up by Charles Bulmer, a wine merchant and early member of the cider-making family, who became a substantial land owner mainly in the Holmer area. In 1833 he bought six strips which had formerly been charity land, given in 1712 to 'support ten poor maids'. The land had been relieved of its charity status and these stones marked Charles Bulmer's new acquisitions.

The churchwardens of Lugwardine put up a number of new stones to mark the parish's charity land in 1870 and they also re-erected some old ones that had fallen. Sadly none of these stones has survived, but the map that was made at the time shows that several of the stones were placed along the sides of the strips as well as at the ends.

More recently the Herefordshire Nature Trust put up several new stones marked 'HNT 1994' to mark the bounds of their strips, thus continuing an ancient tradition of the Meadow.

Stones like those on Lugg Meadow today form the earliest known way of marking boundaries. The first reference to such stones probably comes in the

Fig. 3 Drawings of some dole stones

Old Testament in the Book of Deuteronomy—'cursed be he who removes his neighbour's landmark'. In England, an early reference, in the year 931, recorded that 'twelve stone markers subscribe a meadow' given by the Saxon King Athelstane to the Abbey of Malmesbury.

Later on, manorial court records have many references to mere and dole stones, sometimes stating that they should be set up or checked on but most usually recording that someone has moved a stone illegally. This was a common crime and a 15th-century story recounts how a man on his deathbed, haunted by a huge, fiery stone rushing towards him, confessed that: 'I removed this stone in the field to the intent that I would enlarge my own ground and lessen other mens' ground'.

Although these stones were once so common very few survive today in the country as a whole, but on functional Lammas meadows they are still of importance and Lugg Meadow has far the largest number surviving on any such meadow in the whole country. They have all been accurately mapped and recorded.

The first settlers in New England took the tradition of mere stones across the Atlantic with them from the old country and in 1657 each land owner was ordered to 'bound his land with stakes and stones at the corners'. To do this, at each corner a hole one foot wide was to be dug and the stone laid in it. A stake was then to be stuck in the hole. It is probable that the stone did not project above the ground but could be felt by probing if the stake got broken or lost. It seems that the same system of marking was in use on Lugg Meadow in early days for a sample radar survey in 1994 indicated solid objects in the soil at strip boundaries where an upstanding stone was apparently missing. Excavation of three of these sites revealed, not the remains of large, upstanding stones as expected but something quite different—little cairns or groups of small, undressed, stones. These have been interpreted as an earlier method of marking the boundary of strips and there may well be hundreds of these cairn markers buried all over the meadow which in the past served the same purpose as the New England stones.

(c) Lot-Casting and 'changeable acres'

The division of land in early times aimed to be equitable so that the good and bad parts of a meadow were shared out fairly. To achieve this if a person had several strips in the meadow these did not lie adjacent to each other but were scattered over the whole area.

To allocate the strips even more fairly on many Lammas meadows, and perhaps on all of them in early times, lots were cast each year to determine who should have which strip for that year. The lot casting was not normally done until just before mowing began so that it was in everyone's interest to protect the whole meadow early on while the grass was growing.

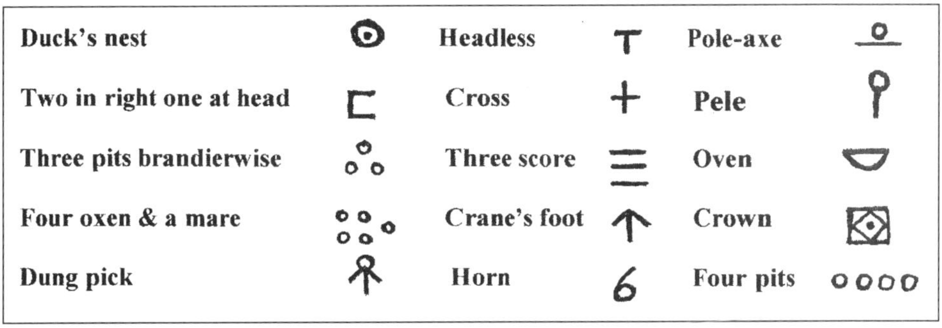

Fig. 4 Some of the symbols used on lots in various Lammas meadows

Various materials were used as lots—sticks, bits of dock root, bits of arrow, apples and leaves are all recorded. These were marked by cuts and holes to form various symbols each being the personal mark of one man and probably also of his family. Some of the symbols used on various meadows are shown with their names in Figure 4 above.

The lots were all put into a hat or bag and someone with no direct interest in the meadow, such as a child or stranger, was called upon to draw out a lot beside each strip as the party moved across the meadow. When a man's lot was drawn beside a particular strip then that strip was his for that year and he at once cut his mark into the ground at its head. Some villages kept a special knife for this purpose. The drawing of lots in this way is a very ancient custom found in other parts of northern Europe as well as Britain.

Most lot-casting came to an end in the 18th or 19th centuries but on one group of Lammas meadows beside the Thames near Oxford it continued right up to the building of the Oxford bypass across the meadow. This so disrupted the organisation of mowing that the lot drawing ceased and the meadow was thereafter cut by a contractor without any reference to the ancient strip pattern. Here they had formerly used cherry wood balls for lot drawing, each with a name on it dating back to the reign of Edward I. These are still carefully preserved but sadly have lost their function. Beside the River Lugg, too, in the 18th century they were drawing lots with names dating back to the same period in the Wergins Meadow in Sutton.

Evidence of lot-drawing on Lugg Meadow itself is not so clear but some parts of the meadow were, in the past, described as 'changeable or running' which meant that the ownership of the strips there rotated yearly. There were at least four parts of the Meadow with blocks of 'changeable strips' and in one of these the practice went on until the 1950s. Here the strips changed hands in an orderly sequence each year until the practice was stopped by mutual agreement among the owners. It seems probable that the 'changeable strip' system replaced lot-casting at some earlier period.

(d) What happened to the Lammas Meadows nationwide and how many functional ones still remain?

In early days most settlements had their Lammas meadow which was highly valued because of its fertility caused by the winter flooding. The meadow was a vital part of the open field system controlled by the manorial court. As this control declined individuals began to exchange strips with their neighbours thus acquiring a block of strips which they would then, illegally, fence off. The court might order the fence to be removed but a weak court could not enforce this and so the land, arable and meadow, began to be enclosed into small, hedged fields.

This piecemeal, private enclosure was often followed by legalised enclosure enforced by Act of Parliament. Once the former common meadows were in private hands and divided up most of the area became pasture land which was grazed all the year round on and off. In this way nearly all the Lammas meadows of the Lower Lugg valley were enclosed, the last in 1804 being the large meadow on the left bank of the river that runs north from Lugg Bridge up to Sutton. The commissioners responsible for implementing this Act complained of the great difficulties caused by uncertain ownership boundaries and 'changeable acres'. They said they could not even find the parish boundaries.

There was talk soon after this of enclosing Lugg Meadow itself but by this time Enclosure Acts were going out of fashion and Lugg Meadow escaped this fate. As a result under the Commons Act of 1965 the Meadow became registered as commonland, but only of course for half the year, from Lammas to Candlemas. This is a very unusual state of affairs and dates back to the origins of the Meadow and the open field system. Most of the registered commonland in the country today derives from the manorial waste lands. These were grazed all the year round in medieval times and so today are commonland for all the year. In contrast registered commons which derived from Lammas meadows were only grazed for half the year and so today are still only commonland for half the year.

Clearly it would be of interest to know how many other Lammas meadows still exist in the country today. and as a result a survey was made in the 1990s. This found that only sixteen functional Lammas meadows still survive in England and of these Lugg Meadow is the largest. It is also the one where medieval methods of management are still the most closely followed.

3

The Historical Record of Ownership of Lugg Meadow

a) The Names given to the Meadow at various times

The earliest recorded name for the Meadow found so far is 'Walney', a name preserved in a charter of the 1180s. This name derives from the Old English name for a spring, a spring that is still present beside the Meadow today. The name 'Walney' remained in use for a long time side by side with the name 'Lugg Meadow' but was mainly used for the northern part of the Meadow. The central part of the meadow was often called 'Kinshey' or 'Kingsey' but gradually the name 'Lugg Meadow' took over entirely from both these other names.

Today Lugg Meadow is known as 'Upper and Lower Lugg Meadow', the two parts being divided by the A438 and these are the names used in this booklet. But this division is a fairly recent development following on the fencing of the road. Before that was done the animals could wander freely across the road and thus over the whole meadow. As a result, earlier on the existing meadow was all called 'Lower Lugg Meadow'. The name 'Upper Lugg Meadow' was used then for the even larger meadow, lying on the left bank of the river, north of Lugg Bridge and running all the way up to Sutton. This meadow was enclosed in 1804.

Two other names for Lugg Meadow have crept into usage in modern times. The first name, 'Lugg Flats', is certainly descriptive of the area but was never used in old documents.

The second name, 'water meadow', is incorrect but its general use has been becoming fashionable in recent years. A true 'water meadow' is a man-made area where, by the construction of dams, sluices and channels, water can be made to flow over the grass at will to increase its productivity. Lugg Meadow, in contrast, floods naturally and should technically be described as a 'flood-plain meadow'.

Water meadows were mainly made in the 17th and 18th centuries and there is a good deal of interest nowadays in their rehabilitation. A number of the flood-plain meadows higher up the Lugg valley were made into water meadows in the 18th and 19th centuries including some on the Hampton Court estate which employed two ‘drowners’ to manage the sluices and water carriages involved in the system. There is no evidence that Lugg Meadow itself was ever made into a ‘water meadow’, indeed with so many owners and commoners involved it would have been difficult if not impossible to lay out and manage such a system.

b) Ownership at the time of Domesday

Given the size of Lugg Meadow and the numerous parts into which it is divided, ownership could obviously be a very complicated matter. However at the time of Domesday, 1086, which is the earliest date for which there is information, the ownership was straightforward. The part of the meadow lying in Lugwardine belonged to the King and the parts lying in Tupsley and Holmer belonged to the Canons of the Cathedral and the Bishop.

Since parish boundaries are thought to be very old indeed, it is probable that the present boundaries were already there at the time of Domesday. We can assume that the areas belonging to the King and to the Church were those shown on Figure 5 which is made up from the parts of the three parishes involved that have land in Lugg Meadow. It was quite normal for a single

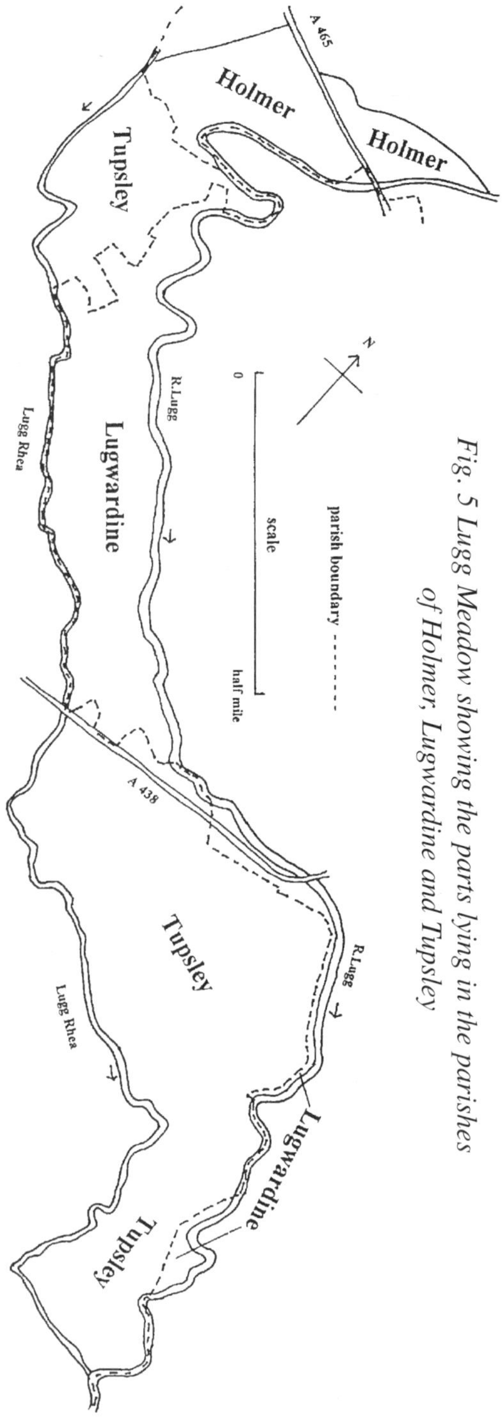

Fig. 5 Lugg Meadow showing the parts lying in the parishes of Holmer, Lugwardine and Tupsley

Lammas meadow to be shared between several parishes because the hay was such a valuable resource that all neighbouring settlements needed to have their share in it.

The parish boundaries in Lugg Meadow form an intricate pattern and in many places are marked by sinuous, ditch-like depressions two or three feet deep. When the Meadow has been flooded these hold water after the floods have receded and show up plainly as they wind across the Meadow. In the past they were known as 'swilleys' and they represent the remains of old water courses. The parish boundary between Lugwardine and Tupsley follows a meandering swilley that can be seen from the A438 as it crosses the Meadow.

Lower Lugg Meadow lies almost entirely in Tupsley but Lugwardine parish has a long, thin strip beside the river called the 'Swilley Swath'. This strip was traditionally the width of one cut of a scythe. As machinery has taken over from the scythe and got larger and larger so the Swilley Swath has got wider and wider. It is always cut and carried first so that it then forms a way by which all those people who own the strips that butt up against it at right-angles can carry their hay without passing over other people's strips. How Lugwardine gained control of this vital strip is not known.

c) After Domesday

After Domesday Book was compiled in 1086 there are increasing numbers of records concerning individual strips and parcels but no overall account was produced again until the 1840s, when the parish Tithe maps with their Apportionments were made. (Figure 7 shows how the Meadow was divided up on these maps into numbered strips and parcels). Unfortunately the Apportionments, though they provide a comprehensive account of the occupiers of Lugg Meadow, do not distinguish the occupiers from actual owners.

As a result the only sure way to identify past owners of any one strip or parcel of the Meadow has been to work backwards from the owners of today to those of the past. This has been made possible in many cases thanks to the quite exceptional number of relevant documents that still survive. Those for the Bishopric estates and for Lugwardine manor are held in the Hereford Record Office and those for the Dean and Chapter and other cathedral bodies in the Hereford Cathedral Archives, housed in the Mappa Mundi building. None of these documents deal specifically with Lugg Meadow in its entirety but a great many are concerned with individual farms and other properties in and around Hereford which owned particular parcels and strips in the meadow. Figure 6 shows the position of these farms which often lay several miles from the Meadow. This unusual situation probably arose because of the very early origins of the Meadow, its relationship with early estates and the exceptional size and value of the hay crop.

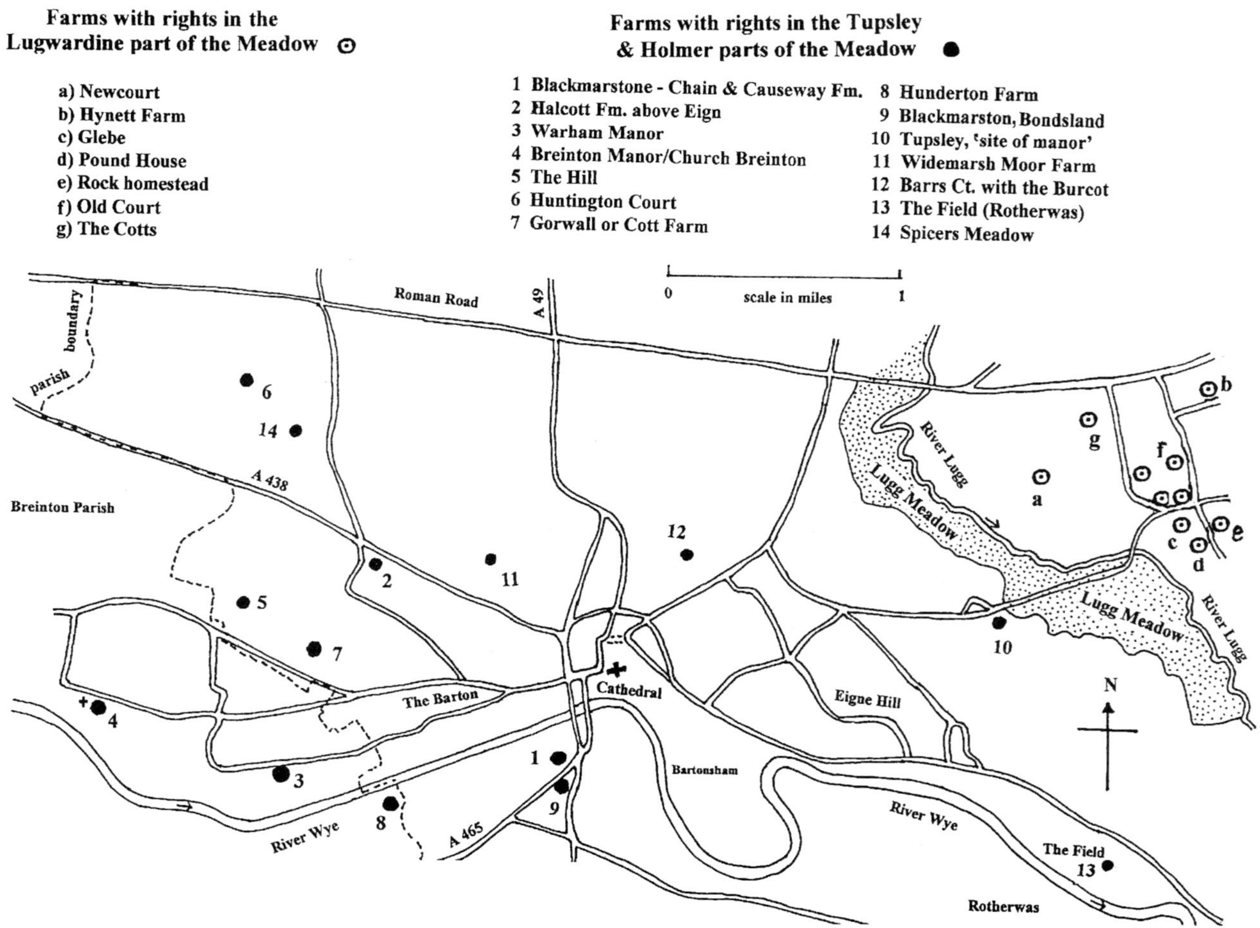

Fig. 6 Map of Hereford city and environs showing farms known to have had hay rights in Lugg Meadow at some period

Working backwards and piecing together the information given in documents, it appears that up to the nineteenth century nearly all the parts of Lugg Meadow in Tupsley and Holmer were owned by the Bishop of Hereford or the cathedral clergy. This of course ties up with the Domesday record and indicates that the church ownership of most if not all of the strips and parcels in these two parishes was continuous from Domesday up to the nineteenth or twentieth centuries. Many of the individual strips and parcels so owned formed parts of the estates with which the cathedral was endowed. These estates are considered to have been acquired well before the time of Domesday but the evidence of their acquisition was destroyed by the Welsh in 1055 together with the cathedral.

The strips and parcels owned by the Bishop and the cathedral dignitaries are marked on Figure 7.

From these early days until the nineteenth century, changes of tenants and information about farms were recorded with increasing accuracy and detail and, towards the end

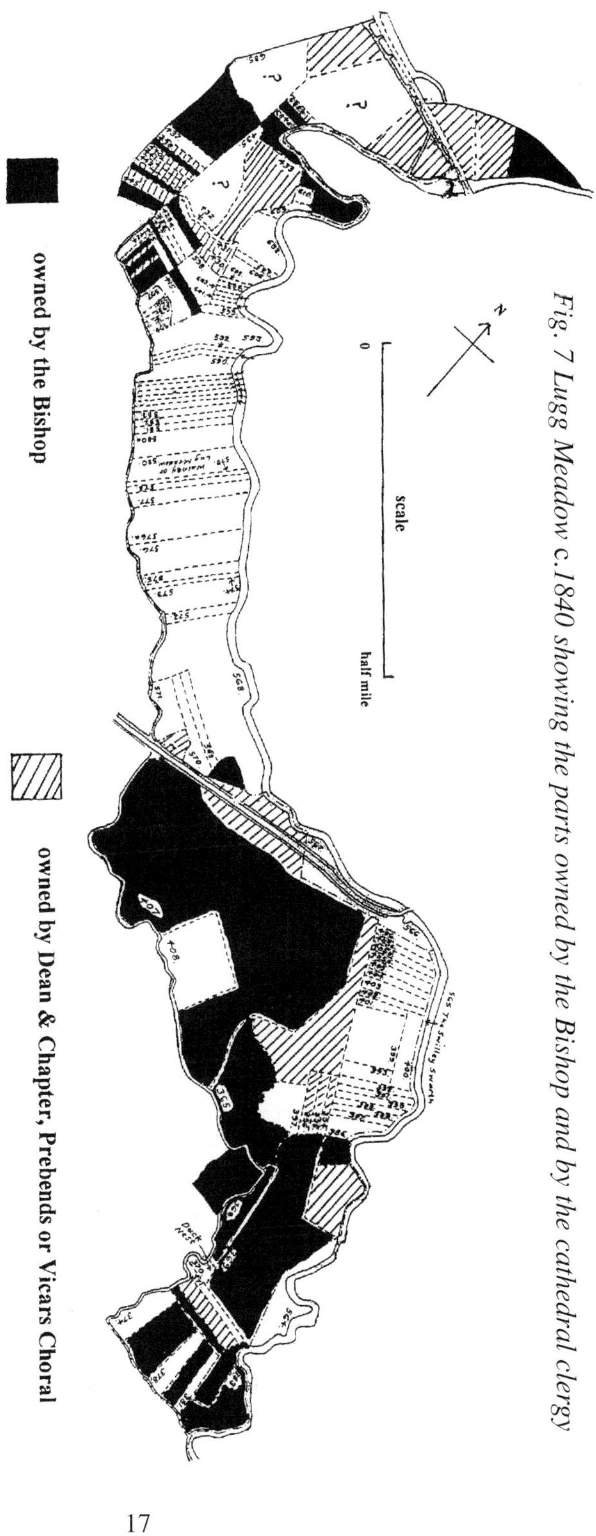

Fig. 7 Lugg Meadow c.1840 showing the parts owned by the Bishop and by the cathedral clergy

of the period, also with good maps. Then, from the end of the nineteenth century onwards, the church began to sell off of its lands.

Lugwardine manor, in contrast to the church estates, passed out of the hands of its Domesday owner, the Crown, fairly early on and thereafter had its own Lords of the Manor based at Newcourt who held their own manorial court. Some of the later Court Books of the manor survive and it appears from these that the Bishop never owned land in the Lugwardine part of the Meadow. Since at the time of Domesday the Lugwardine land was all owned by the Crown it seems that the Bishopric never bought land there at a later date, though other people did.

The Herefordshire Nature Trust bought its first strips on the Meadow, making up eight acres, in 1983 and since then has acquired over one hundred acres.

d) Lugg Meadow in the archives

The first records of the meadow found so far occur in charters in the cartulary of St. Guthlac's Priory where mention is made of 'the meadow of Walney' in 1183-1185. It has been possible to follow up this record and to tentatively identify the actual strip in the meadow today that was once owned by St. Guthlac's.

Very soon after this comes a mention *c.*1290 of Bishop Cantelupe owning three and a half acres in Walney and also a meadow in 'Kingsley'. The Bishop's *Red Book* (1250-1280) lists all his lands and at that time he owned 55 acres of meadow in Tupsley, 53 in Shelwick (Holmer) and 60 in Hampton Bishop. He also held parts of 'Lugg Meadow' which belonged to two other manors situated at some distance from the Meadow itself. One was in his manor of Barton which held eleven acres 'in Walney' and the other at Eaton Bishop which held two acres.

Around 1300 there are several deeds concerning half acres in the Meadow, one of which was called 'Prestheye' and was said to be 'extending to the Bridge of Lugg'. The yearly rent for this was a single rose.

Other early records stored in the Cathedral archives follow:

1386	'2 acres of meadow in Kyngushey'
1417	'a certain meadow in Walney called le Pyk'
1452	'3 acres of meadow in Kyngshey'
1526	'7 acres in Lugge meadow'
1547	'a parcel of meadowland lying in Kings Heye'
1649	'16 acres in the common meadow called Kingsey'

After this references to 'Lugg Meadow' and 'Walney' become more frequent but the use of the name 'Kingshey' comes to an end. It seems very likely that in the earlier times Kingshey was the name for the Lugwardine part of the meadow, the part that at Domesday had belonged to the King, but that after the manor ceased to be in royal hands the name gradually died out. The last use of this name found was in 1733. The name 'Walney' went out of use in the nineteenth century.

(e) How the Meadow was divided up

The tithe map shows how the meadow was divided up between the different owners with the dotted lines representing the invisible boundaries (see Fig. 7). As already described these divisions occur in two basically different shapes, either irregular 'parcels' or long thin rectangular 'strips'. The difference between the two appears to be fundamental and may relate to their origins.

(i) The difference between strips and parcels and their possible origins

The strips are of roughly uniform width and lie parallel to each other. Where they occur they are so regular that those parts of the Meadow must, at some distant time, have been deliberately laid out in this way. At the same time the course of the Lugg Rhea, the stream which bounds the side of the Meadow away from the river and which forms an efficient boundary controlling the movement of stock, must have been deliberately altered. As a result the Rhea has a very unnatural course with several right-angled bends where it bounds the blocks of strips.

Where it has been possible to trace back the ownership of the strips they have been found to have mostly been held by copyhold lease. This was an ancient form of land tenure originally dependant on the custom of the manor and the will of its lord. The tenant was protected in his title by an entry in the court rolls of which he was given a copy, hence the name. When a copyhold tenant died this was recorded in the Court rolls together with the name of the new tenant admitted who was normally the heir. This information makes it possible to trace the history of individual strips backwards though not always to identify them on the ground.

In contrast to the strips the parcels are usually larger and of irregular, curving shapes. How these shapes originated is not known but since many were bounded by a 'swilley' it seems possible that they were first formed as islets in the flood plain lying between the anastomosing (cross-connecting) branches of a much divided river. Part of a description of the lands of the monks of Westminster Abbey in 1065 given in a writ issued by King Edward the Confessor seems to describe just such a scene associating meadows with islets:

> 'with woodland and with open country
> with pasture and with heath
> *with meadows and with aits (eyots)*
> with waters and with weirs'. (Hooke 2000)

(ii) Distribution of the 'Strips'

The part of the meadow lying in Lugwardine parish which is long and fairly thin in shape is basically all in 'strips'. Most of these run across the meadow from the river on the east to the Lugg Rhea on the west.

In contrast the parts of the meadow that lie in Tupsley are made up of a mixture of regular blocks of 'strips' and irregularly shaped 'parcels'. On Lower Lugg Meadow, there are two groups of strips. One lies at the southern end beside the Lugg Rhea. The other lies beside the river and most of the strips here run at right angles to the river though separated from it by the 'Swilley swath'. The strips here were described as 'changeable' which meant that their ownership or tenancy changed from year to year. In the 18th century these were described as 'the common doles', a phrase that implies lot casting or annual doling out.

In the part of Upper Lugg meadow lying in Tupsley parish there are three more blocks of strips running at right angles to each other and lying beside the Lugg Rhea where today the path from Walney Lane enters the meadow. Earlier this area was called Stoney or Walney Stile, perhaps implying a stone stile and bridge over the Lugg Rhea where today there is a concrete bridge.

(iii) Distribution of the 'Parcels'

The 'parcels' lie in Tupsley or Holmer parishes and in contrast to the strips most were held not by copyhold but as detached parts of whole farms which were leased for a period of years. For example the large parcel, 407, was part of Tupsley Court Farm and, very fittingly for a farm situated on the edge of Lugg Meadow, a part of the rent was 'eight wain loads of good, sweet hay' to be delivered to the Bishop's Palace. Several other 'parcels' were parts of farms lying to the west of Hereford and as far away as Breinton.

(f) Tenurial History of the Strips and Parcels

In searching for the original owners of individual strips and parcels it has been found that once the trail leads back to the Bishop or a cathedral body no previous owners can be found—many tenants but no earlier owners—and so the search stops there. It has been found that nearly all the areas in Tupsley and in Holmer, whose history can be traced, belonged to either the Bishop, the cathedral dignitaries, the College of the Vicars Choral or some other body with church connections. A few belonged to either the Rotherwas or the Barrs Court estates but these too may earlier on have been linked to the church (according to Duncumb).

In contrast, in Lugwardine, most of the strips whose history it has been possible to trace, formed either part of the demesne of the lord of the manor or were copyhold of that manor. A number of the strips had however apparently acquired freehold status by the 18th century.

This distribution of ownership found by working backwards from today is thus more or less the same as that known to have existed at the time of Domesday and indicates that the land held by the church in Lugg Meadow at the time of Domesday remained in the same hands right up to recent times, a very remarkable example of continuity. This is shown in the table below which summarises the acreage owned by different bodies in the three parishes.

Owner	Area to the nearest acre			
	Tupsley	Lugwardine	Holmer	Total
Bishop	124	0	3	127
Dean & Chapter and Prebends	18	0	14	32
Vicars choral	22	0	10	32
St. Giles & St. Guthlac	1	0	0	1
Rotherwas & Barrs Court	9	0	0	9
Lugwardine demesne**	0	19	0	19
Lugwardine copyhold ***	0	46	0	46
Lugwardine - poor	1	1	0	2
Lugwardine - glebe	8	2	0	10
changeable strips	12	0	uncertain	12 +
Total	195	68	27+	290+*

Summary of ownership of strips and parcels on Lugg Meadow 1840 and before

** Lugg Meadow, Upper and Lower, contains 326 acres today. This means that some 30 acres are not accounted for in the Table above, largely because the owners of some strips and parcels have not yet been identified.*

*** The strips recorded as Lugwardine demesne are those that in 1840 were in the hands of the owners of Newcourt, ie the lord of the manor.*

**** The strips recorded as Lugwardine copyhold were either identified as such in the Court Books or were in the same occupation as various farms in*

Each strip or parcel has its own individual history. Clearly they cannot all be recorded here but a few are described below:

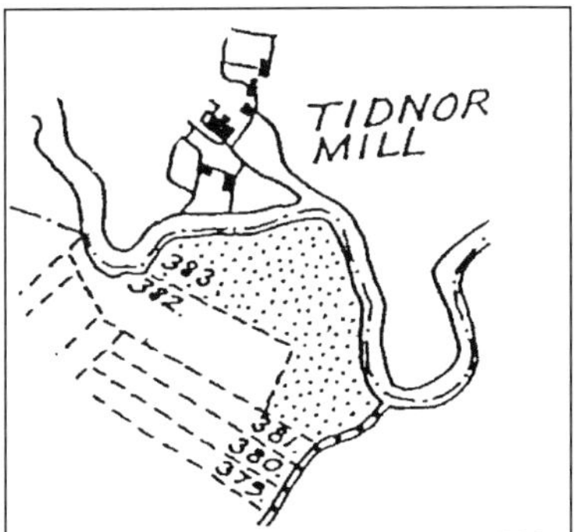

Shooters Hail - number 383

Shooters Hail, number 383

This was only sold by the church in 1952 and with it came no bundle of title deeds as was normal but only a statement to the effect that being Bishopric lands there would be no title deeds. This seems a clear indication that from the time before the Conquest when the Bishopric had obtained its lands, this parcel had never changed hands and so no title deeds had ever been needed.

The name of the parcel probably refers to boats 'shooting' the weir on the river at the nearby Tidnor Mill. The weir would have been made up of 'rhymers' and 'paddles' some of which the miller would have had to remove for a boat to pass through, hence the need for the 'hailing' to give advance notice of the arrival of a boat wishing to pass the weir.

384 'near a place called Tidnor Horn'

number 384 - "near a place called Tidnor Horn"

384 was a relatively large parcel that belonged to the Vicars Choral of Hereford Cathedral and was always refered to as 'parcel near a place called Tidnor Horn', without having a name of its own. It was always a part of Hallcot Farm which lies in Above Eign to the north-west of the city. The surviving leases for this farm begin in 1580 and, as was usual, the phrasing of each new lease was normally exactly the same as that of the one before with only the date and name of the tenant changing. But the lease of 1692, which was granted to Edmund Weaver, is of especial interest because it had an extra phrase added. This called for: 'the inserting [into the lease] of 7 acres of meadow ground in Lugg Meadow (part of this farm) which by the neglect or wilful omission of the clerk was left out of the former lease'.

This phrase shows just how easily a part of Lugg Meadow could be 'lost'. The records do not of course report occasions when 'neglect or wilful omission' was *not* noticed by someone in higher authority but this sort of thing may account for the difficulty found in tracing the history of some of the strips and parcels in the Meadow. Once separated from their farm and forgotten about by their landlord the hay from such parts of the meadow would not go to waste but would be quietly taken over by someone on the spot who of course had no title to it. The phrase 'wilful omission' implies that in 1692 the clerk or his family had hoped to take over this particular parcel.

Simkins Acre, number 398

This name probably refers to some former tenant, Simkin being the diminutive for Simon. The term 'acre' often meant a parcel in the meadow and had nothing to do with the actual area. In 1609 this parcel was leased by the Vicars Choral to Richard Veynal with Warham farm in Breinton. Then in 1672 a Mrs, Veynal was caught 'endeavouring to sell as ye freehold a parcel of ground in Lugg Meadow called by the name of Simkin Acre belonging to ye farm at Warham'. A stop was put to this illegal sale of leasehold land but Mrs. Veynal still continued as tenant.

In 1874 Simkins Acre was leased to F.R. Weg Prosser and he put up stones engraved 'Warham 1857' to mark the boundaries of this very unusually shaped parcel of land.

565 The Swillcy Swarth

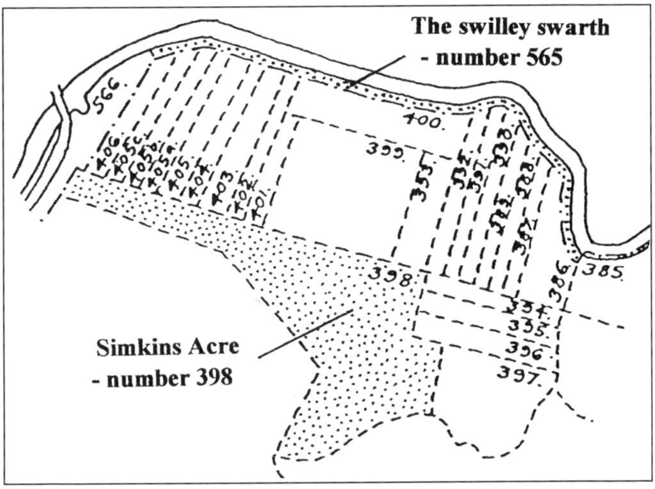

This is a very long, thin strip which lies beside the river in Lower Lugg Meadow. As indicated by the name, it was probably originally one sweep of the scythe in width (each sweep of the scythe produces one swath of cut grass). On the Wergins Meadow, a former Lammas meadow further up the Lugg, the swath beside the river belonged to the Meadsman who always maximised the size of this swath by choosing the man with the longest arms to scythe it for him. The name 'swilley' was used on Lugg Meadow and other meadows nearby to describe an area sometimes washed over by running water, as along the course of a former stream or, as in this case, by the river.

A peculiarity of this strip is that it lies in the parish of Lugwardine while all the rest of Lower Lugg Meadow lies in the parish of Tupsley. Over the course of time this strip has become wider and as it is always cut and carried first it forms a convenient way for the owners of the strips butting against it to carry their hay out of the Meadow.

John Bleeck Lye's strip, number 575

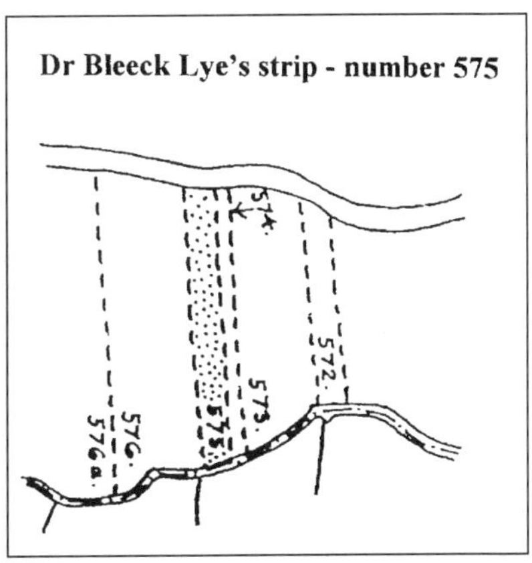

This strip lies in Lugwardine and was bought by Charles Bulmer from a well known Hereford doctor of Castle Street, in 1860. Charles Bulmer was business like and asked for title deeds. All he got was a letter from Dr. Bleeck Lye saying that he had been given the strip by an old friend 43 years before without deeds and no one had ever challenged his right to the land.

This example is quoted here to show how lax procedures for transfer of land were in Lugwardine in contrast to Tupsley and also to show the value of one strip in the Meadow to a professional man who presumably needed the hay to feed the horses that carried him round his practice.

681a The Tithe Acre

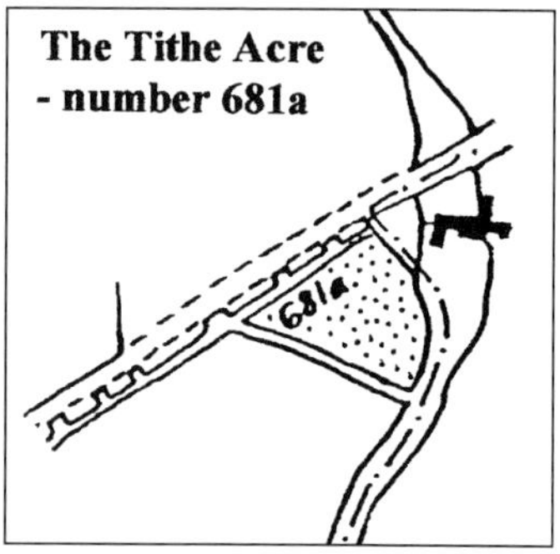

This triangular parcel of meadow, which despite its name is nearly two acres in size, belonged in the past to the Dean and Chapter of Hereford Cathedral and a complete series of leases for the property exists from 1625 until it was finally sold in 1919. It is now in the safe keeping of the Herefordshire Nature Trust.

The name 'Tithe acre' may throw some light on the origin of this parcel. In the past on Lammas meadows, as on all land, the occupier had to pay tithes to the church which were a tenth of what the land produced. This might be wheat, barley, poultry, eggs or all sorts of other produce. In a hay meadow the tithe was levied when the hay had been cocked. Some minion of the church would come to the meadow and take every tenth haycock, checking that by some odd chance every tenth cock was not smaller or more loosely packed than the others. This could delay the time when the hay could be carried from the meadow which, especially in unsettled weather, must have been very annoying to the haymakers. To get over the problem on some meadows, instead of every tenth haycock the tithe owner was given a compact area of the meadow where he could cut the hay himself leaving the rest of the meadow free of tithe. This area was then known as the 'Tithe acre' and this is probably the origin of this parcel of Lugg Meadow.

Every strip and parcel in the meadow has an interesting history behind it and the story to date has been found to involve well over 800 named individuals, mostly from Hereford and around but some from far afield. This, for one area of land, is a very unusual situation and shows clearly the importance in which Lugg Meadow hay was held in earlier days.

g) Before Domesday?

Documentary evidence cannot be expected to take the history of Lugg Meadow back much before Domesday because the destruction of Hereford cathedral in 1055 is considered to account for the almost complete lack of earlier records. However, archaeology could take over where the historical record ends and answer many questions. Already trial cores have been taken from one part of the Meadow and from two metres down organic matter in the soil has yielded pollen grains of many hay meadow plants still present in the Meadow today. Archaeological studies further up the Lugg valley at gravel excavation sites at Wellington and Lugg Bridge are yielding information on the early history of the valley (see section 6) but there is a real need for an archaeological study of Lugg Meadow itself to find out when and how the area first became a hay meadow and what was there before.

4
HAYMAKING

From early times hay, such as that from Lugg Meadow, was the major winter feed for horses, cattle and sheep and was especially needed by farmers for their plough oxen. Later, with the Meadow situated so close to Hereford it was an excellent source of top quality hay for the numerous cart horse stables throughout the city and for dairy farms nearby.

Typically a working heavy horse such as a Shire would be given 16lb. of hay and 12lb. of oats per day while a dairy cow would get 20lbs. of hay per day as its basic ration with concentrates of cereals and protein fed in addition according to its milk yield. A breeding ewe would receive 1-4lb. of hay per day supplemented by swedes or turnips.

Because meadow hay is made up of a great many different plants all live-stock find it much more appetising than hay made from the fewer species that are sown in a temporary grass ley. Additionally the flood-plain meadow hay is especially rich in minerals as a result of the species mix and the rich alluvial soil on which the plants are growing.

Although the nutritive value of hay is at its best when it is made from grasses that have been cut when their pollen has been cast or, using an old term, when they were just past the 'bloom stage' in fact the grasses on Lugg Meadow were usually left a little longer for two reasons. First that by delaying cutting for a week or two the potential crop increased in bulk and secondly at the same time it became more fibrous or 'stemmy' which made the task of cutting it with a

Going to work with scythe, cider barrel and scythe stone

Scythe sharpening with square tapered sandstone

Day 1

Two-man team scything the meadow grass

Day 2

Turning the swath with wooden hay rake

scythe and perhaps more importantly drying it with the sun and wind, that much easier.

Before hay making machinery was invented haymaking on Lugg Meadow would commence in late June and when it looked as though a fine spell of weather was about to commence scythesmen would go down to the Meadow (quite often in small teams) each with his scythe, a fine sandstone for keeping a sharp edge on the blade and his essential fuel for the work, a small wooden barrel usually holding about half a gallon of cider or beer. Solid food was restricted to a modest snack of bread and cheese.

After cutting, the grass would be allowed to lie as it fell 'in the swath' and next day when the dew had dried off it would be turned by hand with a wooden hay rake to allow the sun to dry the underside of the swath. On the third day using a hay fork the swath would be 'tedded' i.e. shaken and fluffed up to allow the wind to move through it.

On the fourth day when the dew had dried off, the hay would be tedded again and turned and by early afternoon the workers, using rakes and forks would gather the hay into rows of small, round 'cocks' each containing up to one cwt. of hay. A skilled worker would build the cock keeping its centre higher than its sides so that any rain water would run off without penetrating the cock to any great extent. Another advantage of cocking was that it enabled a strip of meadow to be cut in two or three sections knowing that the cocked section was secure in case the weather changed. Before carting, the hay in the cocks was spread out for two or three hours in the sun and wind to make sure the moisture content had

Day 2/3
Tedding with hayfork creating windrows. If the weather was 'set fair' the hay could be tedded again and on Day 4 two windrows could be put into one

On Day 5 the hay could then be loaded straight from the windrows

If the weather was 'changeable' on Day 4/5 the hay would be gathered into small cocks holding up to 1 cwt. of hay

The hay would be allowed 'to make' in the cocks before being opened up and carted on Day 7/8

been reduced to at least 20% (judged by squeezing a handful of hay and seeing that it springs back into its original shape on release). It was then pitched into a wagon using long handled 'pitch forks'. The loader, standing in the wagon, received and placed each forkful using a short handled 'loading fork' systematically moving round his load stacking and trampling and keeping the centre full all the time to bind the outside layers together. If the weather was really set fair, instead of putting the nearly made hay into cocks several swaths would be raked together to form 'windrows' for the final drying process. The wagon would then be led between two windrows with pitchers working on each side and two loaders on the wagon.

The full load would then be securely roped before leaving the field. Wagons leaving for Hereford had to be assisted up the steep pitch on what was formerly the main road running beside Lower House Farm with an extra horse, the 'Cock' or front horse which was unhitched at the top and then led back down again by a boy to help the next wagon. This system was still in operation within living memory.

5

THE NATURAL HISTORY OF LUGG MEADOW

a) The different wildlife habitats

Lugg Meadow in common with all the flood meadows in the Lower Lugg valley is underlain by gravels. As a result, once the river level falls after flooding the water drains away fairly quickly so that permanent wet areas are relatively rare, being confined to depressions such as abandoned former river channels.

Apart from the meadow with its levées and ancient channels including the Lugg Rhea there are other wildlife habitats associated with the river channel itself. These include gravel bars over which the water is shallow and relatively fast flowing. These are very noticeable when the river is low and are known as riffles. Between the riffles the bed is inclined to be more muddy, the channel deeper and the rate of flow slower. As it crosses the meadow the river channel is cut into clayey material which, unlike sands, will stand with a practically vertical face. This is most apparent on the outside of bends where the main current sweeps the foot of the bank. On the inside of the bends, however, the banks collapse, sometimes quite suddenly, producing more gentle slopes which become more vegetated.

Part of the Meadow and the whole of the River Lugg, with its bankside vegetation, is designated a Site of Special Scientific Interest whilst the whole Meadow is designated a Special Wildlife Site.

b) Flowers of the Meadow

Because the meadows have enjoyed a very long history of similar management they contain an interesting variety of plants typical of old meadows which are adapted to the changing physical conditions and to the cycle of farming use during the year. It is this great variety of plants, each with a different mineral content, which makes the hay from the Meadow so nutritious and attractive to cattle, sheep and horses.

Understandably the most important of the meadow plants are the various grasses, but some of the more showy flowers will be described first.

The **Fritillaries**, *Fritillaria meleagris*, are probably the best known and most attractive of our flood meadow plants. In mid to late April the large, hanging bell-shaped flowers are amongst the earliest to bloom. In Lugg Meadow the population is unusual as many of the flowers are white. Elsewhere, as in the well known North Meadow at Cricklade, Wiltshire, they are almost all pink/purple, the petals displaying more clearly the chequered pattern. This pattern is the source of the name, Fritillary, which comes from the Latin, *Fritillus*, a dice-box. The 'dice' part meaning diced or ornamented with a chequered pattern; *meleagris*, the second part of the scientific name, describes the same feature as it means spotted like a Guinea Fowl.

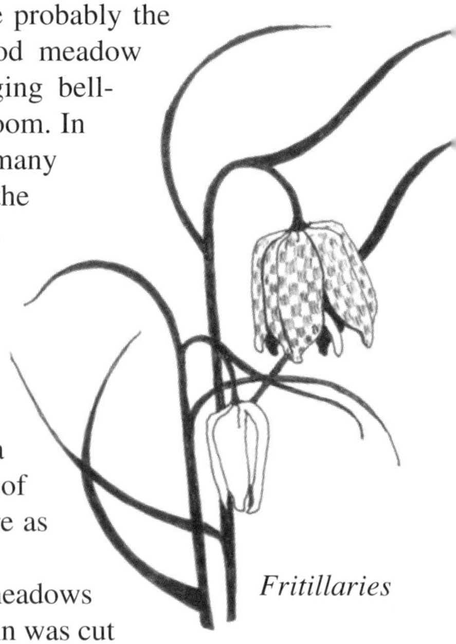

Fritillaries

In northern Europe most of the Fritillary meadows lie by tributaries of the Rhine and before Britain was cut off from the continent by the English Channel, the Thames too was a tributary of the Rhine. It is appropriate therefore that nearly all the British sites for this plant are in the Thames basin, mostly in Wiltshire and Oxfordshire. A flood location is not essential for the plant's survival as it will grow perfectly well in drier sites as it does in many gardens, but it can cope with periodic inundations.

The Fritillary thrives on the haymaking regime. This is because the plant grows from a small bulb which may lie 20 to 25cms. below the soil surface. This, as in all bulbous plants, must be fed by food manufactured in the leaves by photosynthesis. If the bulb is not replenished thus it dwindles away and with it goes the whole plant. The leaves are fine, grass like structures placed alternately up the stem and none forming a rosette at ground level. This arrangement means that the plant cannot grow in short grass that is continually grazed by animals since these regularly remove the leaves as they form. Instead the plant is ideally adapted for the hay meadow regime where the bulb can be replenished by the leaves during the early summer and the leaves will have died back naturally before the hay is cut. By this time the seeds will have ripened, and the activities of haymaking disperse the seeds around. Most of the seeds germinate the following spring and each produces one fine grass-like leaf. These are very hard to see amongst the meadow grasses. The first year only a tiny bulb is made but each successive year the plant makes a few more leaves and a slightly larger bulb until after four or five years the bulb is mature enough to produce a flower.

The population and the area occupied by the Fritillaries in Lugg Meadow have both increased since most of this part of the Meadow was bought by the

Narrow-leaved Water-dropwort

Herefordshire Nature Trust. A count of flower heads in the early years of the Trust's ownership came to a little over 700; the following year over a thousand were seen and a couple of years later counting was abandoned when the number got well beyond 1,500. Lugg Meadow is one of only about a dozen sites in the whole country with over a thousand plants regularly flowering.

The Fritillary is a nationally rare plant and another in the same category which also grows in the Meadow is the **Narrow-leaved Water-dropwort**, *Oenanthe silaifolia*. This is most distinctly a plant of flood meadows which, like the Fritillary, has declined or vanished from many of its former sites where such meadows have been drained, fertilised, treated with weed killer or ploughed, leaving Lugg Meadow a very significant site nationally for this species. This plant is a member of the carrot family and its flowers are normally white but occasionally pinkish. The young leaves are often present when the Fritillaries are flowering and the first flowers may be open before the Fritillaries have gone to seed. The plant is difficult to distinguish from some of its close relatives but the fact that the much divided leaves, including the very lowest, are similar to each other is a good clue to identification as is the thickening of the individual flower stalks when the plant goes to seed. **Pepper Saxifrage**, *Silaum silaus*, is another member of the carrot family which is instantly distinguished from its relatives in the meadow by having cream / yellow flowers.

Great Burnet

Another meadow plant of very special interest is the **Great Burnet**, *Sanguisorba officinalis*. This is a member of the rose family but quite unlike a rose in appearance with its small spikes of tiny dark red flowers. The plant can grow to over a metre in height but the flower spikes are a mere 5cms. or so and can be easily missed. The name *Sanguisorba* means 'absorber of blood' and the whole plant was formerly used for this purpose There is only one small patch of this plant still surviving in the meadow

The **Adder's-tongue**, *Ophioglossum vulgatum*, is present in the meadow in small quantities and widely scattered localities. This is a small fern but very unfern-like in its appearance. It has a single rather plantain-like leaf but this lacks midrib and veins and is referred to as the 'sterile frond'. The separate fertile spike carries the spore bearing structures which appear as tiny brownish bobbles in the upper half of the frond. As the whole plant is green and rarely more than 15 to 20cms. high it is soon overtopped and hidden by the growing grass. The best time to find it is in spring when its rather yellow/green colour should make it easier to spot.

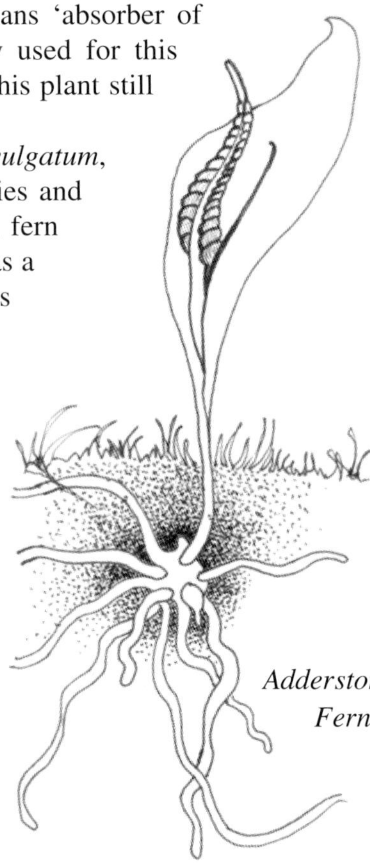

Adderstongue Fern

Most meadows support a number of members of the buttercup family and Lugg Meadow is no exception. In some of the damper depressions the **Marsh-marigold** or **Kingcup** is found while the more familiar Buttercups prefer drier habitats. The first to flower is the **Bulbous Buttercup**, recognised by its turned back sepals, whilst the **Meadow** and **Creeping Buttercups** choose damper places. When the buttercups are in flower the whole meadow is yellow. Still in the same family is the **Wood Anemone** whose occasional presence may testify to the age of the meadow and relative lack of disturbance.

The Daisy family is well represented with such plants as the large flowered **Oxeye** or **Moon Daisy**, **Yarrow**, **Creeping** and **Spear Thistles**, the colourful **Knapweed** and a number of dandelion-like species such as **Hawk's-beards** and **Hawkbits**. The **Autumn Hawkbit** flowers mainly after the hay has been cut. **Dandelions** themselves are abundant and in early summer they colour the whole meadow firstly with their yellow flowers and then with their white 'clocks'. There are many different species of dandelion in the country, a large number of which are confined to particular habitats. Some unusual ones in Lugg Meadow have been identified by an expert as being rare, flood-plain meadow species. These are also found in Picksey Mead, a well-known Lammas meadow beside the Thames near Oxford. One of the Lugg Meadow species still awaits identification.

Yellow Rattle

Other familiar plants which grow in the damper situations in the meadow are **Cuckooflower** or **Lady's Smock**, whose pale mauve flowers are some of the earliest to appear in spring and whose pods are food for the caterpillar of the **Orange Tip** butterfly. Later in the year **Meadowsweet**, with its rather heavy scent, and **Ragged Robin** add colour to the scene. Other plants typical of old meadows are present but less abundant. **Hay** or **Yellow-rattle,** so called because when ripe the seeds rattle in their pod when it is shaken, is an annual species, semi-parasitic on grasses and more often associated with slightly impoverished soils. The iris-like leaves of the **Meadow Saffron** (*Colchicum autumnale*) can be seen in one place in the meadow in spring. These disappear and the purple, crocus-like flowers, do not appear until the autumn. This is not the plant that used to be cultivated to produce the dye saffron. **Meadow Cranesbill** with its large blue flowers provides a splash of colour in a small area.

Meadow Saffron flowers in the autumn

Although the colourful flowers attract the most attention, no account of the plants of the Meadow would be complete without a mention of the grasses. Unlike most of the 'conventional' flowering plants whose bright coloured petals exist to attract insects for pollination, the grasses, being wind pollinated, have no need of petals. Their pollen is produced by the three stamens which protrude from the flowers and release vast quantities of pollen in suitable weather conditions. The windblown pollen grains are then captured by two white, feathery stigmas of another plant which can then produce a new generation of seeds.

c) The grasses

The Bible rightly said ‘All flesh is grass’ since many animals either eat grass directly or prey on others which do so and a large proportion of the food of humans is derived from grass in one way or another. Grazing animals have, it seems, evolved hand in hand with grasses over several millions of years. As a result the grasses are well adapted to being eaten or cut as, unlike other plants which grow at their tips, grasses produce new growth from the base and can therefore survive the continual removal of their upper parts by grazing animals, haymakers or even lawn mowers.

In the Meadow at least twenty different species of grasses have been seen. One of the earliest to flower is the **Sweet Vernal Grass** which contains a substance, coumarin, which gives old meadow hay its wonderful, characteristic scent. **Meadow Foxtail** is also early to flower, starting in April with its fatter somewhat silvery spike-like flower heads and abundant brown stamens. **Timothy** is superficially similar to **Foxtail** but flowers later about June / July. Both these grasses are good fodder species.

Cock’s-foot is a distinctive, tufted coarse grass with flowers in tight clusters at the tips of the branches of its flowering head. The lower part of the stem is flattened which makes it easy to recognise when not flowering. **Meadow Fescue** is a member of the extensive group of Fescues. Its flowering head is loosely branched in a form, present in many grasses, known as a panicle as distinct from a spike. In the Fescues there are only one or two branches arising together from the stem.

The **Meadow Grasses** (species of *Poa*) also have a panicle but with several branches arising together in a whorl. These branches normally alternate, short and long, around the stem and all members of this group have a boat-shaped tip to the leaf. **Smooth** and **Rough Meadow Grass** are both common in the Meadow.

Rye Grass with its spike of flowers is a species that has been much bred for fodder but the original, unimproved form is still present in the Meadow. The **Bromes**, especially **Meadow Brome** are common in the meadow. The name Brome is derived from the Greek word *Bromus*, a type of oat, because of the resemblance of the Bromes to oats. **Meadow Barley** is another wild grass that looks like a cereal, this grows in the damper parts of the Meadow.

(d) Flowers of the River

The river produces a different suite of plants which add interest to a visit to the Meadow. Willow and Alder grace its banks and several ‘water weeds’ grow in the stream itself, the most spectacular of which is **Water Crowfoot**. This is a member of the buttercup family with long stems and thread-like leaves. The long stem can rise and fall with the variation in level of the water whilst the fine leaves offer little resistance to the flow and so escape damage by rapid currents. The flowers are white and can, in good years, provide a stunning display on the

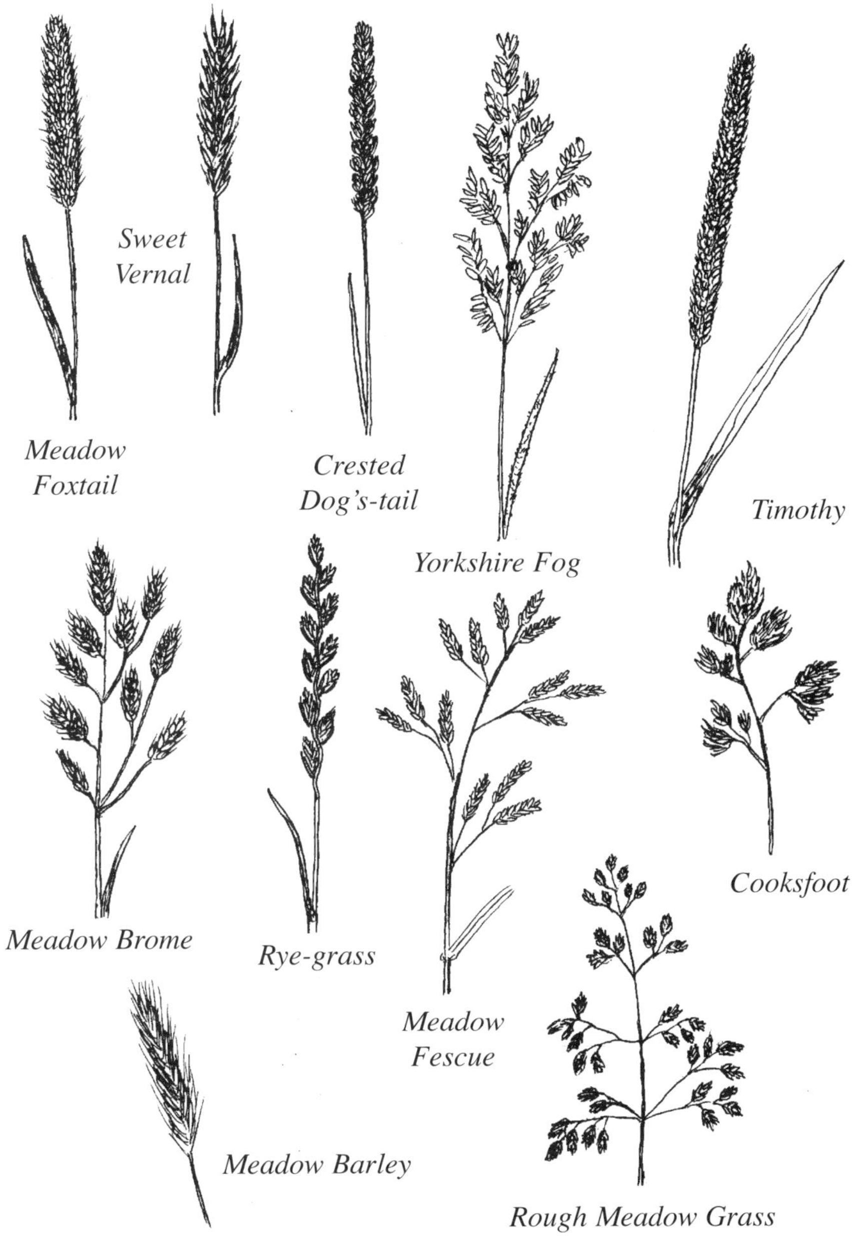

river. The plants root in the gravel riffles and in recent years appear to have suffered a set back probably as a result of mud accumulating in these gravels. This mud is soil washed off former pasture fields upstream that have been recently ploughed right to the river's edge.

Along the side of the channel **Bur-reeds** grow where the bottom is silty and in a few quiet spots there are tall **Rushes** rising up to two metres above the

Flowering Rush and Arrowhead

water. This plant is the one used for seating rush chairs and making rush mats and in the recent past rushes from the Lugg have been cut for this purpose. **Reeds** too can be found in the river and this is the favourite plant for thatching where it grows in profusion. A grass very characteristic of the banks is **Reed Canary Grass** which grows in vigorous tufts which may reach two metres or more. The riverside also supports stands of **Comfrey** and tall spikes of **Purple Loosetrife** together with the yellow **Common Toadflax**. There is even a small stand of the feathery **Meadow Rue** for the more observant visitor.

(A list of the plants found so far in the Meadow is given in an Appendix and if you find any not listed there please let the Herefordshire Nature Trust know so that your find can be added to their records.)

(e) Insects and other invertebrates of the Meadow

Rather little is known about these but **Dragon** and **Damsel flies** haunt the river-side during the summer and **Mayflies** of many species may be seen dancing above the water in due season. Butterflies apart from the **Meadow Brown** are normally rather scarce. The meadow flowers are mostly pollinated by different species of **Bumble bees**. Some rare beetles have been found in the shingle banks by the river. Nothing as yet is known about the fauna of the soil but as undisturbed, old meadow soil is so rare nowadays it must be of interest.

Skylark

(f) Birds of the Meadow

One of the most evocative sounds can be heard in the spring when the **Curlew** returns from wintering elsewhere, probably on coastal mudflats, whilst the

Curlew

Skylark, which has declined so much on most farmland, still makes the Meadow its home, enlivening the air with its song during spring and summer. It may not now, however, breed regularly as in recent years they have not been seen feeding young. The riverside is the most rewarding place for the bird-watcher. Here the sharp whistle of the **Kingfisher** may be heard and with luck a flash of electric blue plumage will be seen as it flies low over the water. **Herons** visiting on fishing trips and **Mallard** may be startled at almost any time of year. In spring the latter can sometimes be seen shepherding their brood as they learn to feed.

Sand Martins nest in burrows in the bank and before the young launch into life in the air, a cluster of heads may be seen in the burrow entrance waiting impatiently for their next meal. **Swallows** and **House Martins** also feed on insects and when these are flying low over the water the birds will be seen in hot pursuit.

The seeds of the **Alders** growing beside the river are especially attractive to **Tits** and

Kingfisher

Sand martin

Kestrel

Goldfinches in the winter and a particular treat is the sight of **Siskins** with even the now rare **Redpoll** joining them. Other winter visitors are the **Redwing** and **Fieldfare**, members of the Thrush family, which come from their breeding grounds in Scandinavia and clear up fallen apples and hedgerow berries but also relish some of the creatures that live in the Meadow soil.

Although not specifically meadow birds many of our songsters can be heard from the Meadow. The strident song of the **Mistle Thrush** chimes out in all weathers from January onwards along with its relatives the **Song Thrush** and **Blackbird**, while the ubiquitous **Robin**, **Wren** and **Chaffinch** nearly always make their presence known. **Yellowhammer** and **Reed Bunting** are sometimes heard and may be seen locally, but both are infrequent. Among the warblers **Chiffchaff** and **Willow Warbler** are regularly heard in the neighbourhood and, in the year 2000 at least, the **Lesser Whitethroat** was heard from the Meadow as it sang quietly in a thorny thicket beside Baynton Wood.

Corncrake

Other birds that always attract attention are the Woodpeckers. The **Green Woodpecker** sometimes feeds on the Meadow probing for insects and the **Great Spotted Woodpecker** visits the larger trees nearby. Among the birds of prey that fly over or hunt in the Meadow the **Kestrel** is perhaps the one most frequently seen followed by the **Buzzard**, but on rare occasions **Peregrine Falcons** have been reported and even more infrequently an odd **Osprey** on its spring or summer

Lapwing or Peewiit

migration. (A little further up the river two **Bittern** skeletons were picked up not so long ago after very cold weather.)

Two species which seem to have been lost, at least as breeding birds, are the **Peewit** or **Lapwing** and the **Redshank** which, within living memory, bred in the Meadow. In former years too the **Corncrake** bred here regularly but for the last time in 1930. This bird, once so typical of English hay meadows, survives now only in some remote parts of Scotland.

Water Vole

(g) Mammals of the Meadow

Mammals on the whole are secretive and nocturnal but **Hares** are reported

Otter

from time to time and the kestrels appear to find plenty of **Voles** or other small rodents. Sadly the **Water vole,** which used to be common here fifty years ago, has gone completely both from here and most waterways in the county It is good to know however that the shy **Otter** frequents the riverside, though very rarely seen.

6
THE ORIGINS OF THE LUGG VALLEY LANDSCAPE

The course of the River Lugg

The source of the River Lugg lies in spring fed marshy ground on Pool Hill in Radnorshire some 17kms. north-west of Presteigne. Its upper course is mainly through uplands with adjacent hills rising to 500 metres. Most of the way to

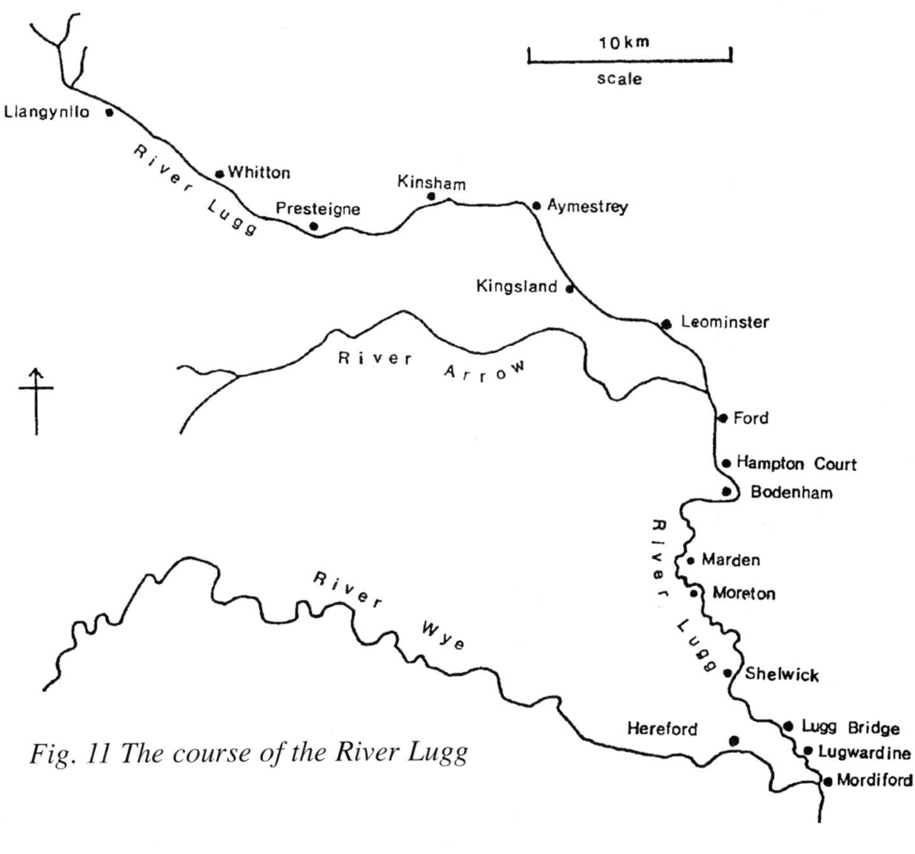

Fig. 11 The course of the River Lugg

Presteigne the valley is broad and open but from there to Mortimer's Cross the river passes through fine limestone gorges at Kinsham and above Aymestrey.

Downstream from Mortimer's Cross the character of the valley changes abruptly as the hills are left behind and the river takes a course mainly through lowlands underlain by marls of Old Red Sandstone age. The relatively easily eroded sediments of these rocks produce the extensive low ground through which the river now flows for most of its journey across lowlands, to its confluence with the River Wye near Mordiford.

Was the Lugg once a much larger river?

Between Hampton Court and Bodenham the river flows in a loop through an open gorge-like valley (described geologically as an 'incised meander'). This meander has been preserved because at this point the river is traversing harder less easily eroded rocks. There is a relationship between the size of a stream and the size of its meanders. The size of the large incised meander near Hampton Court and other similar meanders further downstream on the River Wye suggests that they were originally cut by a river much larger than the present Lugg. Such a river is known to have been the pre-glacial ancestor of the Lugg augmented by the waters of the River Teme, before the latter was diverted to its present course to join the Severn.

Further evidence for the former presence of this large river is provided by the flood-plain. From Mortimer's Cross downwards the Lugg's course follows a very extensive flood-plain, varying in width but sometimes as much as two kilometres wide as in the Marden and Wellington area. But in normal flow the Lugg's channel is abnormally small in relation to the size of its valley. In geological terms such a river is described as a 'misfit'. This discrepancy between the size of the river and the size of the flood-plain provides further evidence that a much larger river once flowed down what is now the Lugg valley.

It is of course the presence of this wide flood-plain that, in the course of time, led to the establishment of the large Lammas meadows in the Lower Lugg valley and the existence of Lugg Meadow itself.

The Flood-plain

Although referred to as a flood 'plain' the surface of the valley floor, despite its appearance from a distance, is far from flat. A walk across Lugg Meadow reveals a number of meandering depressions, some of which represent former courses of the river which have been abandoned and partially filled with sediments. A parish boundary separating Lugwardine parish to the east from the parishes of Holmer and Tupsley to the west follows one of these meandering courses suggesting that at the time the boundary was established, possibly in the Dark Ages (410-700 AD), the river followed a different route.

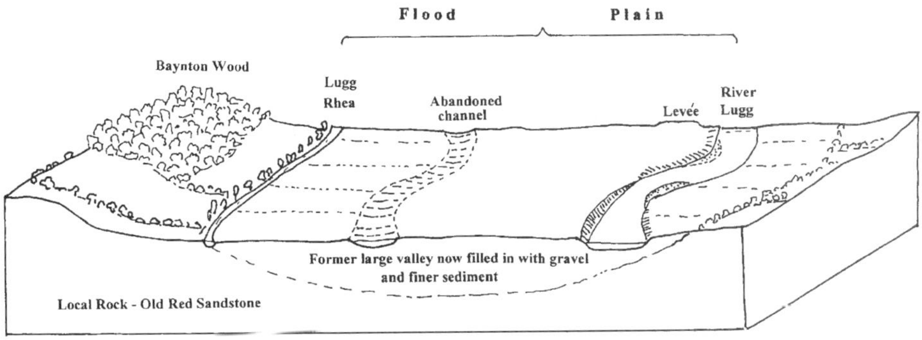

Fig. 12 Sketch block diagram of Lugg Meadow

In times of flood it is evident that there are raised levees or banks parallel with the channel. These are not to be confused with the *artificial* levees which were built beside long lengths of the river in the 1970s. The artificial levees were not built in Lugg Meadow and the small levees beside the river here were formed by natural processes. When the river is flowing at bankfull level it is moving quickly and is transporting large quantities of sediment. This sediment is derived from the banks and bed of the river and the surrounding land. The coarser material is swept along by the fast flowing current and the finer particles are held in suspension in the water. When the sediment charged water overtops the bank it slows down and the coarser material is quickly dropped by the river's edge thus raising the levees a little higher. The rest of the water, with the fine particles still in suspension, sweeps on into the lower land behind the levees forming floods where the water may be static for a long time until the river level drops and the floods subside. Under these conditions the fine sediment settles out slowly and this deposition gradually raises the level of the Meadow by a fine layer of silt after every flood.

Natural streams develop to return the water from the flooded areas to the main channel. The present Lugg Rhea probably originated in this way but long ago had its course fixed and since then has been kept clear by regular dredging to form a drainage channel.

The environmental history of the valley after the retreat of the ice

Seeing the meadows flood, as they do almost annually, and seeing how little the surface seems to rise over the years, leads one to think of the immense time it has taken for the considerable thickness of sediment which now fills the valley to accumulate. It also needs little imagination to realise that the stratified layers which have been laid down preserve much of the environmental history of the catchment area of the river. A glimpse into this history can be obtained by looking into gravel pits such as those at Bodenham, Wellington and Withington. In each of these pits the gravel which is sought is covered by up to three metres of finer sediment which has to be removed before the gravel can be extracted. This overburden contains much information of interest. In some places layers of peat made of the humified remains of contemporaneous plants are preserved representing places where pools, such as ox-bow lakes or portions of old stream channels, have been filled by vegetation falling into them. Provided this plant material was insulated from the air it was preserved and many of the plants can be identified today.

The type and quantity of sediment produced by a stream reflects the conditions within its catchment and by examining this sediment past environments can, within limits, be reconstructed.

The infilling process has taken place since the retreat of the ice of the last glaciation, about 15,000 years ago. The gravels so eagerly sought by the gravel companies form the lowest and oldest layers and a look at the size of the larger of the well rounded pebbles indicates that they could only have arrived in their present position if they had been transported by very fast flowing water. The environment must also have been such that there was a great deal of stony debris available within the catchment.

The ground at this time was sparsely vegetated by plants such as dwarf birch, juniper and wormwood which are found in similar peri-glacial areas at the present time. The rivers of those times must have been quite different from their usually sedate descendants. Snowfall was most likely heavy in winter and, as in Arctic areas today, the streams would have been swollen to torrent proportions as the snow melted in spring. With little vegetation to stabilise the ground there was an abundance of loose debris to be incorporated as sediment and transported down the valley only to be deposited as the velocity of the water decreased.

In addition to gravels and finer sediments being laid down, evidence for contemporary plant life was also incorporated into these deposits. This happened particularly where pools were being colonised by vegetation, some of which has been preserved including the very durable and distinctive cuticles of pollen grains which can be identified under the microscope. Where the 'pollen rain' blown from flowers fell into bogs it was preserved and can today give clear indications of vegetational change thus shedding much light on alterations in the environment.

The period during which the gravels were being deposited by the meltwater streams from about 14,000 to 10,000 years ago is known as the Late Glacial, and by the latter date it had come to a relatively abrupt end, possibly in the space of about fifty years. The summer temperature which had been around 10°c, rose to nearer 16°c. This climatic amelioration allowed plants to grow which could not previously have survived, and with their arrival the whole appearance of the landscape altered. One of the first changes was when birch trees, *Betula pubescens*, rather than dwarf birch, *Betula nana*, began to invade in quantity and what had been a tundra with scattered trees developed into birch woods. The birch was an admirable coloniser as it could withstand the cold of peri-glacial winters, spread easily with its small, winged seeds and thrived in the bare ground where competition was limited.

Between 10,000 and 8,000 years ago deciduous woodland was established containing trees still familiar to us today The dominant birch was replaced by Scots pine but this in time was replaced by hazel followed by oak, elm, alder and eventually lime which is the most warmth loving of our forest trees.

Under the cover of the trees with their dense ground flora the bare, easily eroded ground was stabilised and the formation of forest soils began. The regime of the river also stabilised as the vigorous snow melt periods became a thing of the past and by 9,000 years ago the more sedate, meandering channel of our river had become established.

In these conditions the supply of sediment was minimal so that between 7,000 and 5,000 years ago a very much reduced accumulation took place on the flood-plain. The 'pollen rain' of this period was very largely supplied by trees whilst the amounts of grass and other herbaceous pollen fell to a minimum indicating that the flood-plain was covered by forest.

The start of agriculture

This state of affairs changed again about 5,000 years ago when there was a sharp fall in tree pollen, notably that of elm, followed by a decline in lime and accompanied by an increase in the pollen of grasses and herbs including that of weed species such as plantains and cereals. This sequence is taken to indicate the arrival of humans with a form of settled agriculture. The decline in elm could have resulted from the use of the young, nutritious leaves as fodder and could also be related to clearance for crop growing as could the later decline of lime. Both of these trees thrive in rich soils and may therefore have been selectively removed by early farmers. The decline in tree pollen was complimented by an increase in the pollen of herbs and grasses representing the change to a more open landscape, whilst the arrival of plantains which grow well in rich, cattle poached ground indicates the presence of farm animals. The arrival of farming with its associated forest clearance and disturbance led to erosion of the soil and increased sediment carried by the river so that the flood plain deposits also increased rapidly.

Lugg Meadow itself is a relatively blank area for archaeological knowledge but a small, pilot environmental study carried out in 1996 by the County Archaeological Service identified pollen grains of plants still typical of the Meadow today at a depth of two metres. A more detailed study would be of great interest.

Higher in the Lugg valley at Marden more extensive archaeological work has found layers of peat incorporated in the deposits and these contain alder logs suggesting that alder woodland (known as *carr*) was a significant feature of the flood plain vegetation. Plant remains including pollen found in higher, and therefore younger levels of the soil include nettle, elder, blackthorn, bramble, dock, dogs mercury, thistle and water plantain. These were later joined by buttercups, sedges, stitchwort, St. John's-wort, willowherb, woody nightshade, mint, gypsywort, rushes and several other plants of damp habitats. This collection of plants is indicative of those which may have grown around a meadow such as Lugg Meadow but the history of its use as a Lammas Meadow with its distinctive system of tenure enters the realms of documented history and has been discussed in earlier chapters.

7
CONCLUSIONS

The importance of Lugg Meadow for nature conservation results from its long continuity of management as a hay meadow and this has resulted from its ancient status as a Lammas meadow.

Hay meadows are the habitat that has suffered the greatest loss in recent years as a result of modern agricultural needs and methods. Over 96% of the meadows we used to have in the country have gone and with them have gone the flowers, insects, birds and other wildlife typical of the old fashioned hay meadow. Lugg Meadow however has survived and come down to us from Domesday times with its landscape, its wildlife and its management unchanged in essentials and with large parts of its history recorded in detail in the cathedral archives stored in the prestigious Mappa Mundi building.

Somehow, probably because it is flat and because it is still actively farmed, there has been a failure to appreciate what an amazing and unspoiled place Lugg Meadow is. Hereford city is lucky to have this wide expanse of ancient meadowland with its beauty, its wildlife and its history right on its doorstep.

8
VISITING LUGG MEADOW

There are two public footpaths that cross Upper Lugg Meadow and four access points (see map).

One of these paths runs roughly beside the River Lugg between the two main roads the A465 and the A438. This gives good views of the river itself as well as of the Meadow.

The second public footpath runs from the bottom of Walney Lane across the Meadow towards the river and links up with the first path. A third public footpath starts in Tupsley beside Lower House Farm and after crossing a meadow belonging to the Herefordshire Nature Trust climbs the hill above Baynton Wood and then drops down to join the footpath at the bottom of Walney Lane.

By combining parts of these three public paths with a permissive path, a pleasant circular walk can be made which starts at Lower House Farm in Tupsley. This attractive early 17th century timber-framed farm house is the Headquarters of the Herefordshire Nature Trust. The wildlife friendly garden and parts of the building are open on weekdays. Information about nature conservation in Herefordshire, leaflets about Lugg Meadow and Lower House Farm, cards, bird food and other goods are available.

The circular walk starts by passing through a kissing gate just below Lower House Farm and then runs beside a newly planted mixed-species hedge and an orchard. Part of the orchard is old but part is made up of young apple and perry pear trees of various old fashioned varieties

After crossing a stile the path passes through a meadow owned by the Trust. Just above the path and parallel with it are two long, thin flat areas visible in the grass. These may be 'lynchets' and if so represent the remains of medieval arable farming in one of Tupsley's former large, open fields called 'Aylestones Field'. The path then climbs the hill and comes out onto some Hereford city amenity grassland above Baynton Wood. Views of Lugg Meadow are particularly interesting from here when the hay is being cut and the pattern of ownership strips shows up. Baynton Wood is a fragment of ancient woodland which

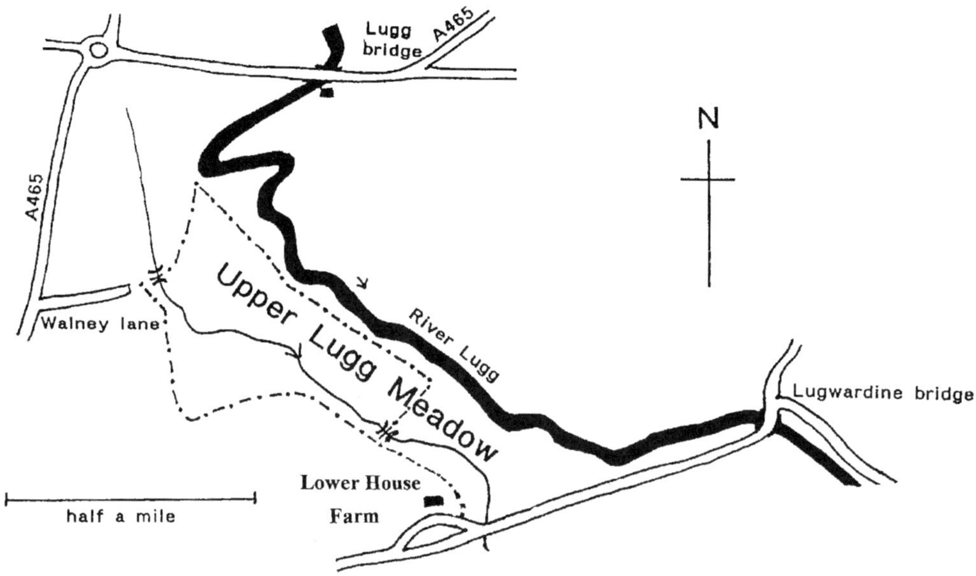

has survived because it grows on a steep slope and it still has bluebells and some small-leaved lime trees growing there.

The path then drops down hill and joins the path from Walney Lane to cross the Lugg Rhea on a footbridge. Following the path straight across the Meadow towards the river it passes beside a newly erected dolestone inscribed HNT 1993 marking a boundary of the Herefordshire Nature Trust but also inscribed LHC on one side and SHDC on the other. This was the boundary between the Liberty of Hereford City and South Herefordshire District Councils, set up before the two bodies became merged in the new Herefordshire Unitary authority.

On reaching the path parallel to the river turn right (south-east) and follow this path until you are nearly opposite Lower House Farm again when a Permissive path will be found leading off on the right back across the Meadow. This part of the Meadow is owned by the plant conservation organisation Plantlife. The path leads to another bridge over the Lugg Rhea which was put up recently by the Nature Trust in memory of a former chairman. From here the original footpath beside the orchard leading to the kissing gate can be regained.

While walking on the Meadow PLEASE keep to the footpaths and when the hay is growing walk in single file so as not to batter down the valuable crop and spoil it.

PLEASE keep dogs under control (on leads) at all times of year so as not to disturb the birds. Some of these nest in the long grass in spring and in winter others feed on worms and insects in the soil. Continuous disturbance by the free-ranging dogs of walkers makes life very difficult for them and may drive them away from the Meadow completely.

Appendix: Plants of Lugg Meadow (excluding waterside plants)

Adder's-tongue	*Ophioglossum vulgatum*
Barley, Meadow	*Hordeum secalinum*
Barley, Wall	*Hordeum murinum*
Bent, Creeping	*Agrostis stolonifera*
Bent, Common	*Agrostis capillaris*
Bird's-foot-trefoil	*Lotus corniculatus*
Brome, Barren	*Anisantha sterilis*
Brome, Soft	*Bromus hordaceus*
Brome, Meadow	*Bromus commutatus*
Burnet-saxifrage	*Pimpinella saxifraga*
Buttercup, Bulbous	*Ranunculus bulbosus*
Buttercup, Creeping	*Ranunculus repens*
Buttercup, Meadow	*Ranunculus acris*
Cat's-ear	*Hypochoeris radicata*
Cinquefoil, Creeping	*Potentilla reptans*
Cleavers	*Galium aparine*
Clover, Red	*Trifolium pratense*
Clover, White	*Trifolium repens*
Cock's-foot	*Dactylis glomeratus*
Couch	*Elytrigia repens*
Cow Parsley	*Anthriscus sylvestris*
Cowslip	*Primula veris*
Crane's-bill, Cut-leaved	*Geranium dissectum*
Crane's-bill, Meadow	*Geranium pratense*
Crested Dog's-tail	*Cynosurus cristatus*
Crow Garlic	*Allium vineale*
Cuckooflower	*Cardamine pratensis*
Daisy	*Bellis perennis*
Daisy, Oxeye	*Leucanthemum vulgare*
Dandelion	*Taraxacum sp.*
Dock, Curled	*Rumex crispus*
False Oat-Grass	*Arrhenatherum elatius*
Fescue, Meadow	*Festuca pratensis*
Fescue, Red	*Festuca rubra*
Field Horsetail	*Equisetum arvense*
Foxtail, Marsh	*Alopecurus geniculatus*
Foxtail, Meadow	*Alopecurus pratensis*
Fritillary	*Fritillaria meleagris*
Goat's-beard	*Tragopogon pratensis*
Greater Burnet	*Sanguisorba officinalis*
Hawkbit, Autumn	*Leontodon autumnalis*
Hawkbit, Rough	*Leontodon hispidus*

Hemlock	*Conium maculatum*
Hogweed	*Heracleum sphondylium*
Knapweed, Common	*Centaurea nigra*
Lady's Bedstraw	*Galium verum*
Marsh-Marigold	*Caltha palustris*
Meadow Saffron	*Colchicum autumnale*
Meadow Vetchling	*Lathyrus pratensis,*
Meadow-grass, Rough	*Poa trivialis*
Meadow-rue, Common	*Thalictrum flavum*
Meadowsweet	*Filipendula ulmaria*
Mouse-ear, Common	*Cerastium fontanum*
Oat-grass, Yellow	*Trisetum flavescens*
Pepper-saxifrage	*Silaum silaus*
Plantain, Ribwort	*Plantago lanceolata*
Primrose	*Primula vulgaris*
Ragged Robin	*Lychnis flos-cuculi*
Ragwort, Marsh	*Senecio aquaticus*
Rye-grass	*Lolium perenne*
Salad Burnet	*Sanguisorba minor*
Sedge, Glaucous	*Carex flacca*
Sedge, Hairy	*Carex hirta*
Selfheal	*Prunella vulgaris*
Silverweed	*Potentilla anserina*
Sneezewort	*Achillea ptarmica*
Sorrel, Common	*Rumex acetosa*
Sweet Vernal Grass	*Anthoxanthum odoratum*
Sweet-grass, Floating	*Glyceria fluitans*
Thistle, Creeping	*Circium arvense*
Thistle, Spear	*Circium vulgare*
Timothy	*Phleum pratense*
Tormentil	*Potentilla erecta*
Trefoil, Lesser	*Trifolium dubium*
Vetch, Tufted	*Vicia cracca*
Water-dropwort, Narrow-leaved	*Oenanthe silaifolia*
Water-dropwort, Tubular	*Oenanthe fistulosa*
Water-starwort, Common	*Callitriche stagnalis*
Wavy Bitter-cress	*Cardamine flexuosa*
Wild-oat	*Avena fatua*
Wood Anemone	*Anemone nemorosa*
Wood-rush, Field	*Luzula campestris*
Yarrow	*Achillea millifolium*
Yellow-rattle	*Rhinanthus minor*
Yorkshire Fog	*Holcus lanatus*

Glossary

Aftermath: The grass that grows after the hay has been cut. It can either be grazed or cut again as a second crop of hay.

Candlemas: Feast of Purification of the Virgin, February 2nd.

Common Field / Open Field: A large area of open, arable land subdivided into strips in individual ownership but all managed in common.

Common meadow: A meadow divided into strips owned by individuals during the hay growing season but with grazing in common after Lammas day (synonymous with Lammas Meadow).

Copyhold: A an ancient form of land tenure dependant on custom and the will of the lord of the manor. A tenant's title to his land was a copy of the entry in the court book of the manor.

Demesne: Land retained by the lord of the manor for his own use.

Dole: A strip or portion of a common meadow.

Dole stone: Stone marking the corner of a dole.

Drowning: Deliberately flooding a meadow with river or spring water to encourage early growth of grass as in a water meadow.

Ea: Old English for river, see also *Rhea*.

Flood-plain: All land adjacent to a water course over which water flows at times of flood.

Flood-plain meadow: A meadow situated in the flood-plain of a river or stream that floods naturally.

Hay: Long grass that has been dried.

Hayward: An officer of the parish looking after the stock on the common meadow.

Intercommoning: Several settlements having common rights, usually for grazing, on the same land.

Lammas, Loaf mass: August 1st, the day when the first loaf made from the new corn was taken to church to be blessed.

Lammas Meadow: A Common meadow opened for communal grazing on Lammas Day.

Lot meadow: A Common meadow where strips or doles are allotted annually by casting of lots.

Lynchets: See under *Strip lynchets*.

Lugg Rhea: Small stream bounding Lugg Meadow on west side.

Meadow: Grassland managed by cutting annually for hay.

Meadsman: The officer of the parish in charge of the hay-making on a Lammas Meadow.

Mere stone: Stone marking a boundary, alternative name for a dole stone.

Open Field: See *Common Field.*

Oxbow lake: Lake formed by a loop of a meandering river that has been cut off.

Paddle (of a weir): Post with a plank on its lower end, moved to open a gap in a weir.

Pasture: Permanent grassland grazed on and off all through the growing season.

Rhea: Strictly means 'at the river' but in the Lugg valley seems to be used for a watercourse beside a meadow. See also *Ea*.

Rhyme: Moveable post forming part of a weir and supporting the paddles.

Riffles: Gravel bars in the bed of the river.

Strip lynchets: Open field strips on a slope where they appear as a series of horizontal terraces.

Swath: Ridge of grass/hay left lying after being cut by a scythe.

Swilley: Linear damp depression marking former watercourse.

Waste: Inferior land occupied in common mainly as rough grazing, belonged to the lord of the manor.

Water meadow: Meadow to which water is conducted by specially constructed channels from which, by the use of sluices, it was made to flow across the grass and return to the river by more channels.

Windrow: A row of hay formed by shaking up (tedding) a swath to maximise the drying process by wind and sun.

Further Reading

The books and papers listed below provide general background reading or are relevant local studies.

Aston, Michael, *Interpreting the Landscape*, Batsford. 1985

Aylmer, Gerald and John Tiller (eds.) *Hereford Cathedral, A History*, The Hambledon Press, 2000

Brandon, A., *Geology of the country between Hereford and Leominster*, HMSO, 1989

Brian, Anthea, *'As to the River Lugg'- its vanished mills, broken weirs and damaged bridges*, TWNFC, 1994

Brian, Anthea, 'Lammas Meadows - a survey of their present day survival with special reference to the Lugg Meadows', *Landscape History*, volume 15, 1994

Brian, Anthea, 'The allocation of strips in Lammas Meadows by the casting of lots', *Landscape History*, volume 21, 1999

Dinn, James and Rebecca Roseff, 'Alluvium and archaeology in the Herefordshire valleys', *Alluvial Archaeology in Britain*, Oxbow Monograph 27, 1992

Herefordshire Field-name Survey with the Tithe maps for the parishes of Holmer, Lugwardine and Tupsley, Woolhope Club, Archaeological Research Section, Hereford

Hooke, Della (ed.), *Landscape - the richest historical record*, Society for Landscape Studies. Supplementary series, 2000

Lugg Meadow, leaflet by Herefordshire Nature Trust, 2002

Lugwardine in the nineteenth century by Lugwardine Historical Society, 1988

Pearson, Elizabeth and Rebecca Roseff, *Paleoenvironmental reconstruction at the Lugg Meadows, Hereford: Pilot study* , HWCC County Archaeological Service internal report, 428, 1996

Rackham, Oliver, *History of the Countryside*, Dent, 1986

Sheppard, Jane E., *Origins & evolution of field & settlement patterns in the Herefordshire Manor of Marden*, Occasional Papers No.15, Dept. of Geography, Queen Mary College, University of London 1979

Stone, R., *Lugg Meadows, Hereford - Report on an archaeological investigation*, Hereford Archaeology Series 203, March 1994

Thorn, Frank and Caroline (eds.), *Domesday Book, Herefordshire*, Phillimore, 1983